ORDINARY ENGLISH SPEAKING MEN, EXTRAORDINARY BEAUTIFUL WOMEN, TEACHING ENGLISH IN JAPAN

CHRISTOPHER KONA YOUNG

Copyright © 2006 by Christopher Kona Young.

All rights reserved. No part of this publication can be reproduced, stored in a retrieval system, or transmitted in any form or by any means, electronic, mechanical, photocopying, recording or otherwise, without the prior written permission of the publisher and/or author.

While every precaution has been taken in preparation of this book, the publisher assumes no responsibilities for errors or omissions, or for damages resulting from the use of information contained herein.

Some characters and events portrayed in this book are fictitious. These names, characters, places and incidents either are the production of the author's imagination or are used fictitiously and any resemblance to actual persons, living or dead, events or locales is entirely coincidental.

First Edition 2006
First Printing 2006

ISBN: 978-1-4116-6892-8

Printed in the U.S.A.

Dedicated to my family and friends

CONTENTS

INTRODUCTION..9

PART I

1. ORDINARY ENGLISH-SPEAKING MEN, EXTRAORDINARY BEAUTIFUL WOMEN 12

    Are there ordinary English-speaking men dating extraordinary beautiful Japanese women?...14

    Are there many English-speaking females dating Japanese males?

    Are Japanese women beautiful?...18

    The English Effect: Who are Fearless Ferrbal, Mary Edgeminded and Cylent Sam?...20

    Examples of How Crude changed without changing himself....28

    Opinions of Men and Women...30

    Who Walks First...35

    Who Pays...35

    Awesome-looking women/men...36

    Which Country to Live In...36

    Meet the Folks...37

    Matchmaking...37

Weddings...37

Good Points...39

Dating Percentages ...40

Summary...42

PART II

2. AN AUGUST DAY 43
3. Q&A 50

   What kind of Education Do I Need?...50

   Do I Need Experience?...51

   Do I Have to Speak Japanese?...51

   Is Japan Expensive?...52

   Can I Get a Job?...53

   What are the good and bad points of being an English Teacher?

   What makes a good teacher?...54

   What kind of person would enjoy living and working in Japan?55

   What kind of person leaves soon?...56

   Should I apply from the U.S. or apply in Japan?...57

   What kind of person will a school hire?...58

   Tell me more about the students...59

   Do I need a Visa?...61

PART III

4. A JOB HUNTING STORY ...62
5. STEP 1 – THE BIG DECISION ...71
6. STEP 2 – PACK LIGHT, PLAN WELL ...74
   Where...74
   When...74
   Pack...74
   Budget...75
7. STEP 3 - MAKE 2 RESERVATIONS AND SOAR TO THIS LAND...77
8. STEP 4 – ON MONDAY, BUY THE ENGLISH NEWSPAPER...79
   Before the Interview...79
   During the Interview...80
   Do's...80
   Don'ts...81
   After the Interview...81
   Other Sources...82
9. STEP 5 – IF WE PERSIST, THE OFFER WILL COME...84
   Student Strong Points...85
   Student Weak Points...85
   Common Mistakes...86
   Grammar Points...86

Impromptu Lesson Plan...86

Impromptu Lesson Example...87

10. STEP 6 – FIND AN APARTMENT 89

Rental Example....90

PART IV

11. SQUID AND MAYONNAISE PIZZA 92

My Top 5 Recommendations...96

Restaurant Do's and Don'ts...98

Intriguing Vending Machines...99

Libation...99

My Top 5 Drinks...100

12. MINI-MINI SKIRTS ……………………………………..101
13. DEFINITELY NOT A LAW SCHOOL …………………….103
14. THE HAND THAT GROPES AND OTHER SEXUAL SUBJECTS…………………………………………………...106
15. TEACHER/STUDENT PROFILES, SURVEY AND TYPES…...110
16. THE RESTROOM KNOCK…………………………………...117
17. MOVIES BY ANOTHER TITLE ...……………………………119
18. WHICH IS MORE PRIMITIVE CHICKEN OR FISH? . ………121
19. CAPSULE HOTEL ……………………………………….123
20. THE CASE OF THE MISSING WESTERNERS……………..126
21. JAPANESE ENGLISH ...…………………………………..130
22. IMAGE OF AMERICA…………………………………………134

Questions I have been asked as an American...136

23. HAWAIIAN EATS..138

PART V

24. THE FUTURE..140
25. REASONS TO STAY FOR A WHILE............................142
    We can go...142
    The Job...143
    Money...143
    Satisfaction...143
    Working Environment...144
    Good Management...145
    Budget...146
    Travelling...148
    Mount Fuji...150
    Hot Spring Baths...150
    History...151
26. EMBRACE THE CULTURE...154
    Embrace the Culture Test...155
    6 Ways to Enjoy the Culture...155
27. CONCLUSION...157

INTRODUCTION

Going abroad to live for a short time can enhance our perspective, our sense of being and our lives one-hundred-fold. This experience is priceless and one that can only be received by traveling. I think everyone would enjoy living in another country for an extended period of time because of the following reasons:

- It allows us to see how differently life is lived in other countries.
- We can eat genuine ethnic food and learn to speak another language.
- It gives us the opportunity to empower our international intelligence and learn about what others think about America – some people like America and some don't.
- We can build our financial intelligence by being our own CEO and earning, spending and saving in another country based on our own decisions.
- We are able to strengthen our emotional intelligence by dealing with an unfamiliar environment in a land a long way from home.
- Living abroad in the Internet age and in a high-tech country like Japan makes life very convenient. We can conduct our personal

business such as banking and transacting with most companies. We can instantly email our family or read the hometown newspaper online or on our cell phone.
- We can make friends from other countries. I have met teachers from Australia, England, South Africa, New Zealand, Canada and many U.S. States. Besides Japanese people, I have talked to people from Korea, Vietnam, China, Mongolia, Thailand, Laos, and Brazil.
- We are able to learn more about ourselves and help others.

Living abroad can be a way to learn, build skills, gain experience, meet others, earn money, broaden our horizons, help others and enjoy life.

I chose Japan because of the following reasons:

- Safety - It is one of the safest countries in the world.
- Modernity - It is a high -tech country.
- Economy- It is the second strongest in the world.
- Cleanliness - some public areas don't have trashcans because it reduces litter? It works.
- Good people – In many respects, some people are kind, non-confrontational, quiet, nonviolent, non-intrusive and polite.
- Food – shrimp tempura, ramen noodles and Japanese hash beef.
- History and culture – temples and shrines abound everywhere, with unique festivals in every town.

- Mount Fuji- anyone can climb it in the summer.
- Hot spring baths- they are healing, healthy and soothing.

    I want to share some of the experiences I have had while living in Japan, and help and encourage those who are thinking of teaching in this country. My life here has been spent in the Tokyo metropolitan area and relates to my personal experiences and interaction with Westerners from many countries as well as many Japanese people. I have written about my beliefs and observations based on my surroundings and the people that I have met. Many people here have been kind enough to provide their thoughts and ideas for this book, and I am thankful to them.

    I have tried to summarize certain beliefs and tendencies based on the peoples' actions and opinions and do not generalize about everyone. I hope you are able to visit or work in Japan, or that this book in some way provides you with something funny, insightful or refreshing.

PART I

1

ORDINARY ENGLISH- SPEAKING MEN, EXTRAORDINARY BEAUTIFUL WOMEN

A curious phenomenon has been observed here in Japan. The phrase 'opposites attract' has taken on a whole new meaning. What does it mean? Simply put, there are ordinary English-speaking men successfully dating extraordinary beautiful Japanese women. This curiosity has been written about in the media and talked about for some time. Back home we might jokingly refer to such couples as modern day reenactments of 'Beauty and the Beast'. The graphic terms and lengths in which this phenomenon has been discussed attests to both its prominence and persistence. Some critics have commented that these guys wouldn't be able to get into the ballpark let alone reach first base with women under normal circumstances back home. (Wait a minute, are they talking about me?) It has been joked about that Japanese women don't see these travelling Romeos as they really are as surely they would be able to distinguish the frogs from the princes and run away.

Foreigners in Japan are few in numbers and benefit from a simple imbalance in supply and demand. In other words, Nippon being a homogeneous country, with only 1% of its population foreign, more Japanese people want to socialize with foreigners than there are foreigners to go around. Furthermore, in regards to native English-speaking foreigners, western culture and English seem cool and fashionable, and native English-speaking foreigners from affluent countries are consequently respected and desired whether or not they are inherently deserving of such.

If we ate a tuna sandwiches everyday, we would probably get tired of them and would enjoy eating pizza or noodles for a change. Most Japanese meet and talk to other Japanese everyday, and as a result, some of them enjoy meeting foreigners. For them, it is kind of like travelling to another country without leaving home or having a dash of exoticism at ones doorstep. Having foreign friends and talking about other countries and cultures can be very revealing and interesting. By contrast, America has so many different kinds of people; it is normal to meet people from other ethnic groups. For people from such cosmopolitan countries, it is hard to imagine always living in a country that is 99% non-foreign.

At the same time, we realize that not all locals seek to meet foreigners. The Japanese people we meet tend to have an international mindset, like to travel and are not ultra-conservative. They are very hospitable and enjoyable to meet. But back to the question at hand.

Are there ordinary English-speaking men dating extraordinary beautiful Japanese women?

Yes, there are some relationships like this. Western men in general seem to have some social advantages, and therefore beautiful Japanese women may date ordinary Westerners because:

- There are very few English-speaking men in a country that has come to be obsessed with the English language, English-speaking countries and English-speaking people. Just speaking English seems to be attractive over here. It is the new romantic language.
- The definition of attraction may be different in Japan. For example, a physique considered scrawny in the west may be attractive in Japan therefore 'smaller' (framed) men may be more preferable or acceptable here, while 'bigger' men may be preferable in the West. ' Small' is fine here.

- Nippon is a very traditional country, where a big age difference between a man and a woman has been historically acceptable. Therefore the female in any given relationship may be young and attractive (beautiful) and the male older and no longer so attractive. Age difference is no problem.
- For those whose agenda is so inclined, could a Western boyfriend double as an English teacher? How about a boyfriend/teacher combo?
- Some Japanese women might be looking for other qualities such as personality, kindness and humor and are not so concerned with youth and physical attractiveness.
- Other women might simply want something different in a country of sameness – a foreigner. And since English is required in school in Japan and becoming more and more important in the business world, it is easier to communicate in this specific international medium. Hence, some Japanese women are more receptive to native English-speaking men.
- Some Westerners are aggressive enough or feel comfortable enough to approach and pursue Japanese women. Maybe it is harder and more intimidating to pursue beautiful women back home. Western magazines say that men may also be afraid of beautiful women (in their own country). Also, it is very competitive back home. There is no shortage (?) of rich, smart, handsome guys back on the ranch in the homeland. (My female colleague thinks there is a shortage.)

- Certain women here are receptive enough to meet these men. Japanese women are marrying later. Many of them are not rushing in to a traditional marriage. Newspapers say that they want to work, travel, shop and enjoy life. Others see a foreigner as an escape to another world. And why not choose a world that is equal to or more affluent than Japan which generally applies to most English-speaking countries. Many of them don't want to tell mom and dad that they will get married and will have to move to some unfamiliar country so this naturally inclines them towards English-speaking men who may take a bride back to their own country.
- A language barrier can be an advantage. Eloquence and smooth pickup lines are not necessary between two people who can't speak fluently in each other's language. There is more tolerance for misunderstanding; in fact the inability to precisely communicate often allows each party to wallow in romantic surrealism, thus fueling the attraction. All Japanese study at least 6 years of English, which covers only the basics. Maybe a romantic word such as, 'Food?' and lots of gestures will suffice as an effective dinner date proposal.

But, are there many English-speaking females (western women) dating Japanese males?

Yes, there are some relationships like this but not as many as the Western male- Japanese female relationship because:

- In Japan, there are more English speaking males than English-speaking females in the teaching community. It is easier for males to travel alone, and Japan is a male-friendly country so it is attractive to males.
- Because of the language barrier, it may be harder for Japanese males to approach Western females and start a conversation in English. Westerners are not required to study Japanese in school, so usually the Japanese male must strike up a conversation in English. In order to make any kind of proposal and risk failing, men in general need a lot of confidence and not having confidence in the language compounds the challenge. If the challenge seems too great, the Japanese male is much likelier to opt for a date in his native language.
- Some Western women come to Japan with their boyfriends or their husbands.
- Western magazines say that dialog is very important for females in a relationship and lack of it may be a hindrance. I haven't met many Western females that speak fluent Japanese. On the other hand, some Japanese women may be willing to sacrifice fluent dialog in order to have a relationship with a foreigner.

- It is possible that Japanese men are used to a man-first culture and western women are used to an assertively feminist society so some conflicts are possible. For example, "who walks through the door first', 'who carries the groceries', 'who pays for dinner' and 'who is the boss' may all engender conflict.
- The average height of the Western female is higher than the average height of her Japanese counterpart and may be a discouraging factor as many men and women prefer that the man be taller than the woman.
- As liberal as the west may be, not many Western women that I have interviewed will actually approach and try to pick up Japanese men, especially when men, in general will approach them. It is easier to be approached than initiate contact and risk rejection.

Are Japanese women beautiful?

Japanese women have enjoyed a favorable worldwide reputation historically. This image has carried over to today and while they retain many of the attributes of their grandmothers, they are changing and adapting to the westernization of their culture. As a result, they have a combination of traditional and modern values. It is impossible to generalize about a whole group yet at the same time it is reasonable to express certain observations. So while we cannot describe all Japanese women, based on a poll of western men in Japan, they believe that some Japanese women seem to have certain tendencies. These include being:

- Very feminine (soft high voice, dainty gestures, submissive downward glance)
- Very clean (showering and bathing once or twice a day, with each bath and shower lasting up to an hour)
- Always fashion conscious (for themselves and their partners. Your humble author by contrast thinks this. If I don't dress well, I get scolded. But my T-shirts with holes are favorites. They are comfortable).
- Deferential to men (In Japan, men traditionally walk ahead of their women and lead the conversation)
- Shy or giving the impression of shyness (some Japanese women say they are shy or say they have to be shy)
- Non-confrontational (the use of indirect disagreement, preferring not to say 'No' in a frank manner, and rarely any yelling)
- Shade-seekers as they avoid the sun. Some use the umbrella to protect their skin.
- Careful of what they eat (the food in Japan is low-fat and healthy, which contributes to their appearance. They have become taller but obesity rates remain low).

One living in Japan would probably observe that some Japanese women are like this while others are not at all like this. Some of them are quite the opposite. For example, some Japanese women like to suntan and some are very bold. All individuals are different. Really? How about in a society like Japan that values conformity?

Some of the traditional tendencies may have arisen from Japan's unique history and culture, and it is this uniqueness that has shaped traditional and modern gender roles. It is easy to see that gender roles here are different from the Western world. Just as Japanese's perception of Westerners is curious, Western men's perception of certain Japanese women is equally curious. Do reality and perception equate?

Without knowing the answer, perhaps this can be said about perception. While it is true that all individuals are different, certain Western men living in Japan who were surveyed, perceive that the tendencies listed above make some Japanese women beautiful and popular.

The English Effect: Who are Fearless Ferrbal, Mary Edgeminded and Cylent Sam?

It is the year 3009 A.D. The world is one big nation and very few people speak English. English-speakers called 2009ers or foreigners are transported by time machine from the year 2009 to the year 3009 to teach the 3009ers or indigenous ones how to speak English.

In the year 3009, there are all kinds of 2009er men. Some have higher qualifications such as PhDs and MBAs while others were taxi drivers or sales people back home. These qualifications or work history seem to be largely irrelevant in social situations here.

Some 2009er men in 3009 have steady girlfriends, and some are just dating while others are involved with computers, careers, travelling, art, sports or history. And then there is the coarse playboy, Mr. I. M. Crude. Back in 2009 this mediocre player had the mentality of a gigolo but was only marginally successful. Women back in 2009 didn't quite see him as a prize. But now he has come to 3009.

It all started on the time machine to 3009. On the long trip to 3009, he fell into a deep sleep and had a strange dream. In this dream, Crude met a middle-age man leaning against a lone tree on the top of a hill.

'Who are you?" queried our coarse playboy.

'I am the King of Couth,' whispered the man wearing dark glasses.

'Why am I here?' asked our uncouth player.

His royal couthness took off his shades (in a really couth motion by the way) and explained.

'Since you are an English-speaker, I will grant you special powers. I will give you a magic cell phone. However…'

'But I'm already groovy,' interrupted our dreamer as he woke himself up (in a really uncouth drooling snort, by the way).

Our awkward playboy shrugged off the dream, arrived in 3009 and went to his pre-arranged apartment. His two new 2009er roommates welcomed him.

The first one had an interesting habit, and as a result, was appropriately known as Cylent Sam. Cylent knew that there were some situations in which it was advantageous to blend in with the 3009er crowd. He didn't enjoy being asked for his foreign ID card nor did he enjoy being stared at. Therefore, on his days off, Cylent wore a T-shirt, jeans, dark glasses, a cap and never spoke and, as a result, everyone in public thought he was a regular 3009 person. Cylent believed that foreign guests were sometimes treated differently; either better or worse than indigenous citizens and there were times when he wanted to be treated like any other person. Other times when authorities or thugs were about, looking homogeneous was wise.

Since 3009 is a highly automated time, Cylent could get through a whole day without talking by using machines such as the ATM, train ticket machine, soda-vending and food-ordering machines in restaurants. On the weekend, he could move around in complete anonymity.

The second roommate was a classy groundhog who worked as a golf pro. Despite being a bad golfer, 3009er country club gladly hired him because he could speak English. He seemed to be very popular with the 3009er ladies. On the other hand, the boorish playboy, Mr. Crude hung out with foreigners and was treated accordingly. Sometimes he made an obscene remark and got slapped in the face.

One night after partying at the 2009er bar, Crude walked slowly home. With fresh slap marks on his cheek, he felt depressed and wondered why he couldn't be like his popular golfer roommate. When he arrived home he was shocked by what he saw. All of his roommates' things were gone except for the roommates' one cell phone, cap and dark glasses. Why did his roommates suddenly move away?

The next day I. M. went to 3009er country club to look for his golf pro roommate. When he arrived at the club, he saw a 3009 female being molested at the practice range. Crude rushed towards the female to help her and as he prepared to call the police using his golfer roommate's cell phone, he flipped it open and it caused the 3009 female golfer to go into a spell. Her eyesight became 20/20, her hearing became clear, her sense of taste, smell and touch became refined and her judgement became excellent. As a result, her perception of Crude began to change.

In her now crystal-clear vision, Crude's forearm tattoos and goatee disappeared and his entire body became covered with fur, his leather jacket fashioned into a plaid, buttoned-up golf shirt and his cigarette breath became peppermint fresh breath. His dark glasses changed into black-rimmed reading glasses.

His cigarette turned into a metal driver and his crudeness became classy until astonishingly as the spell took full effect, it was like total metamorphosis had occurred. Then and there he strutted, the total antithesis of his former self, awesomely transformed from coarse playboy into classy groundhog – sophisticated, huggable and polite – Golf pro Fearless Ferrbal. He took the metal driver and pummeled the groper until he ran away.

"You are my hero, Mr. Fearless," the 3009 female sighed.

Crude was shocked. He now realized that there had never been any classy golfer roommate. He, I. M. Crude was his classy, groundhog roommate, Fearless Ferrbal. They were the same person. Fearless was very puzzled.

What is it about 3009er country club? Why did the King of Couth give him this power? Well here in 3009, it is a different time thus it is a different story. The answer to lonely female golf students seems to have arrived and Fearless may feel as though he has arrived in a temporal paradise of social redemption. While he was usually rude, loathsome and apathetic, the magic cell phone made him courteous, fluffy and brave.

In the year 3009, there was a country club for foreigners known as Traditional Country Club where things were quite different. Females usually fought off their own gropers. Because of security 'jam boxes', the magic cell phone didn't work so females' senses remained unchanged. Therefore, when I. M. was at 2009er country club, he was never a hero. He was still Crude.

At 3009er country club known as Progressive Country Club, the magic cell phone always worked, and therefore he was Fearless Ferrbal.

The magic cell phone gave him three powers: 1) telepathic chameleon – he was able to change females perception of him so that each individual 3009 female golfer was able to see him as her favorite furry animal (therefore, he was always perceived with a different appearance depending on the female's thoughts, sometimes he was a koala, sometimes a panda, other times a groundhog (as above) or a bear etc., 2) polite – he became classy and well-mannered, and 3) sense evil – he could sense where a crime was taking place and he would wildly 8-iron the punk and save the girl. At 3009er country club, he had many female fans but he ignored them all. There was only one he loved.

Our newly minted hero fell in love with his best golf student, the beautiful Ai-chan. Over the next few months, they walked along the beach during sunset, went to late-night movies and had long romantic dinners. They were very happy together and for just a second, Ferrbal considered proposing. Could Ai-chan be the one? Alas, he couldn't make a commitment and to make matters worse, her parents didn't accept him. They were concerned about various issues including Ferrbal being a foreigner and they didn't want her to travel to another time period. With mixed feelings and much regret, she tearfully left him. He was heartbroken.

To forget his sorrow and vent his anger, Ferrbal went from one golf student to another breaking hearts, often multitasking with several girls. His new powers made him cocky and condescending so sometimes his date dropped him faster than a two-foot putt on a downhill green. But what did he care. Too many girls, too few waking hours. He ate, slept, dated and bought wedges. Our sultan of swing met girls at the golf shop, at the golf range and at the, windmill hole of the mini-golf course? Often he unabashedly boasted of his exploits and expeditions to anyone that would lend an ear. He looked in the mirror and was glad that finally females could see him, as he truly was – a creature for all enlightened women. He was irresistible, insatiable and unstoppable.

All heroes have a nemesis and unfortunately, our soldier of splendor was no exception. He was always wary of his archenemy – the voluptuous Mary Edgeminded. She was 29 years old and her two younger sisters and best friend were already happily married. Mary subscribed to Pretty Future Bride magazine and she wanted Fearless to be her future groom.

Ms. Edgeminded was very dangerous because she had many powers. For example, she was beautiful, independent, intelligent, really nice, successful in her career, could cook Pacific Rim cuisine and could tune up her car's carburetor. Furthermore, Mary knew of a substance found deep in the mines of sub-Saharan Africa; a weapon so potent that it could stifle Fearless' superpowers – the diamond ring. Whenever Ferrbal walked near a jewelry store, which had a special sale on diamond rings, he felt weak. Despite being ungainly, Fearless used his fleet-footedness to escape any 'engagement' with his nemesis and her sparkling weapon.

3009er country club was often pestered by Ferrbal's most evil enemy, Dirty Villain. Dirty would grope young women in the clubhouse or on the golf course then escape into the golf courses' rough. Although Fearless was always able to throttle this persistent pervert, Dirty Villain was always able to get away.

Fearless' best friend, Connie Confident came from 2009. Golfer Ferrbal often confided in Connie about his inner fears of commitment, family and lifelong work. She could see that he subconsciously wanted a family but that he hid behind his polar facades.

Back in 2009, Fearless had worked as a supervisor in the claims department of an insurance company in a northeastern metropolis. He had graduated from a West Coast university. On weekends, he had frequented the singles bars and on Sundays, he had ridden his motorcycle through the large park or had shot pool in the pool hall. He had not been without some social skills and had usually dated two or three girls at one time.

He had often worn his girl-hunting uniform of a leather jacket, moussed hair, expensive watch, dark glasses, cigarette and top-of-the-line cologne. In 2009, some women had liked him and some had not as he was an overt player type and always on the prowl. The pre-studster had the attitude but not all the charms of a true Casanova. Now he has brought his rap to 3009.

There have been a few Fearless Ferrbals. They arrive, love and leave. Every so often a new Fearless Ferrbal comes to 3009. He is not such a bad guy in many respects, maybe even kind of a nice guy sometimes. It is just his curious social behavior that draws the ire of others and causes the eye-rolling. He wasn't fully understood back home and now he has found his destiny... at least until he returns back to his world. Let's not cast the first stone, as all foreigners, men and women alike have benefited to some extent from this unsolicited perception-altering phenomenon. For now, he has his reality and we have ours.

What about Cylent Sam? I. M. Crude went out into public and searched the crowds looking for roommate Cylent Sam. Then he got lucky. While walking along the sidewalk, Crude saw Cylent inside a store. I. M. looked again and realized that he was looking at his own reflection in the glass window. Crude was wearing Cylent's cap and dark glasses. I. M. Crude was also Cylent Sam. With much to ponder and a journey to continue, Cylent simply turned and walked and disappeared back into the mass of humanity.

EXAMPLES OF HOW CRUDE CHANGED FROM COARSE PLAYBOY TO FERRBAL, CLASSY GROUNDHOG WITHOUT CHANGING HIMSELF

HIS ACTION	AT 2009 TRADITIONAL COUNTRY CLUB His Date said:	AT 3009 PROGRESSIVE COUNTRY CLUB His Date said:
Slurps noodles	'How rude!'	'How polite!'
Walks through door first	'Whatever!'	'Manly!'
Pays for dinner	'I can pay half!"	'Gentleman!'
Eats curry stew with a spoon	'Here's a fork!'	'Good etiquette!'
Doesn't attempt to open taxi door for her	'Well?'	'Knowledgeable!'
Reads MotoBike Magazine	'Put that away!'	'Intellectual!'
Chugs beer	'Drunk!'	'Assimilates!'
Tells Date's dad- 'I like drinking'	(Date's dad-Frowns)	(Date's dad-Grins)
Flirts with waitress	'Jerk!'	'Jerk!'
Grunts 'Un' instead of 'Yes'	'Excuse me?'	'Knows colloquial language!'
Discusses billiards	Yawn…	'Eloquent!'
Beats up muggers	'I can do it!'	'My hero!'

| Says 'Hey baby, are you diggn what I'm spittn?' | 'I'm not your baby!' | 'English! Classy!' |

CONCLUSION

2009 A.D.

As the airplane's seat belt sign blinked off and a passenger stood up, Mary Edgeminded woke up. She was in the middle of an impossible dream about the year 3009 and a time machine. What?!? Was all of this all just a dream? Were Fearless Ferrbal, I.M. Crude and Cylent Sam just a creation of her subliminal thoughts?

Mary had just finished graduate school and was flying to Japan to start a new job, and was wondering whether this dream was somehow related to her new life. No, it was just a weird dream; such outlandishness could never be connected, she concluded. Noodle slurping, polite? Ha! As she drifted back to sleep in the plane's darkened cabin, she noticed a dirty leather jacket slipping off the empty seat next to her.

The End

OPINIONS OF WESTERN WOMEN

- A female who has a Japanese boyfriend said that communication breaks down because linguistic nuances and unspoken aspects of language are not readily comprehendible between the couple.
- Another females said that some Japanese men are shy and the female will probably have to make the first move.
- One young woman mentioned that she preferred Western males because they didn't pay an excessive amount of attention to their hair and fashion.
- One opined that western women are looking for security and (in this lady's case) intent upon returning to her home country. These two objectives can usually be reached in a relationship with a Western man. She said most Japanese men have more career opportunities in Japan and find it harder to move to a western country. She commented that some Japanese women on the other hand might be willing to take a secondary role and move to a foreign country where the Western man is at home and has an advantage. She added that the less social life a Western man had back home, the more he will see Japan as a 'candy store' and chase many receptive girls.
- An Australian woman said she asked a Japanese male acquaintance to have coffee with her because she wanted to practice her Japanese. She waited for an answer and glanced down at her watch and when she looked up, he was gone. She felt he was very shy.
- One woman felt that many Japanese girls adhere very much to the Western concept of feminine beauty. On the other hand, she said that

her young Japanese male friends enjoy their own style (which is attractive to Japanese females). She continued to say that a Japanese girl is not so different in fashion and style than certain Hollywood female movie stars whereas a young Japanese man is not so different in fashion and style than Japanese male movie stars.

OPINIONS OF JAPANESE WOMEN

- A flight attendant said that she led a elder Japanese male passenger to his seat and he complained because he said males should walk first. She apologized and walked behind him. She said she prefers the female-first culture.
- A full time working wife said she does all the housework and cooking for her Japanese husband and 25 year old son.
- A 30-something wife said her Japanese husband does half the housework.
- A young store manager commented that western men compliment females and Japanese women appreciate that. She said that Japanese women believe Western men are chivalrous.
- A young office lady opined that she preferred Japanese men because she didn't have confidence in speaking English.
- One woman mentioned that she liked it when Western men cooked for her.

- A thirty-something housewife said that her husband doesn't want her to work because he wants a smiling wife to greet him when he comes home from work. She said this arrangement agrees with her.
- One discouraging fact stated by a young lady was that Western men living in Japan almost always return to their home country and that the relationship would likely end as a result.

OPINIONS OF JAPANESE MEN

- A middle-aged executive mentioned that western women are pretty and would like to date them but they have personalities that are too strong for him.
- Two men agreed that western women are wild and exciting and their behavior is acceptable and interesting but the same behavior wouldn't be acceptable in Japanese women.
- A man said that he liked blue-eyed western women but they are hard to meet.
- One fellow stated that he would want a relationship but communication is a barrier.
- A single working man said that western women are too aggressive compared to Japanese women. He added that etiquette is required to relate to Westerner women and it is troublesome whereas 'lady-first' etiquette is not needed to relate to Japanese women.

OPINIONS OF WESTERN MEN

- A man who has been dating many females said that each Japanese female is different but often seems receptive.
- One guy stated that he preferred well-traveled, international Japanese women because there would be too many cultural differences with a very traditional one.
- Another male mentioned that Japanese women have very strong relationships with their mother. Daughters feel an obligation to help or listen to their mothers.
- Japanese women are not as torn between choosing career and being a wife said one man. He said according to their way of thinking their roles are more traditional.
- A married man stated that western men don't know what they are getting into. He said that Japanese women are feminine and make dinner but that the western man must also play the traditional male role too and change the light bulbs and do other 'mans' chores. Lastly he voiced that moving to another country can be very rough for the Japanese wife if she can not assimilate well.

Some Japanese men that I have met work very hard and often come home near midnight. The trains at night are crowded with late returning businessmen. "Karoushi" is the term that means death from overworking and it sometimes happens here. Some jobs have 20 hours shifts such as security guard jobs.

Certain Japanese females are tolerant and stronger than they first appear. I have heard of a woman who was being sexually harassed on the train and just tolerated it for 20 minutes rather than make a scene. When returning to a friend's house, I saw a man and his dog. The dog was doing its business in front of the house. When I told the owners wife and their daughter, they just cleaned up the mess and didn't confront the dog owner as I had expected they would. Their strength seems to be in their tolerance.

Western men and women that I meet in Japan seem to be similar to each other. They are independent, have a job, and do housework. They are very supportive and understanding of each other. GET OUT! … No, really.

WHO WALKS FIRST

When I approach a door with my wife, I usually wait for her to go through first and she usually waits for me to go first in this man-first country so we are both end up waiting at the entrance. Usually I gesture for her to go first but other times I give up and just go first. I wonder, who should walk first?

WHO PAYS

Japan is a traditional country and men usually have a higher salary so men usually pay for dates. Many Japanese women also expect Western men to pay in the same manner and therefore Western men must be prepared to foot the bill. The offer to share the check is sometimes just a formality. Men should politely decline and pay the entire amount.

AWESOME-LOOKING WOMEN/MEN

When male newbies arrive here their jaws drop and the say 'Wow look at that beautiful women there and there and there'. After a few years, the veteran mumbles to himself 'There's another awesome-looking woman (yawn, ho hum).'

On the other hand, the attractiveness of Japanese men has not gone unnoticed by some Western women. Sometimes a female teacher has commented that she looks forward to meeting her favorite private male student. But girl, he is only 17!

WHICH COUNTRY TO LIVE IN

The biggest concern for an international couple is which country to live in. It is very difficult in some cases to say goodbye to your home country forever. Someone has to leave their family, friends and familiar surroundings. Someone has to give in and make a sacrifice. Yet it has been done many times especially in countries of immigrants, America, England, Australia, New Zealand and Canada.

MEET THE FOLKS

Generally dating couples don't meet each other's parents unless they plan to marry. The usual purpose of meeting the parents is for the couple to seek permission to get married. The parents may have questions for the couple and the meeting helps clear any issues. Getting permission is not always easy and there are times when the parents do not agree and then the relationship may be in jeopardy. Couples usually wait and ask again later. For international couples, it just gets more complicated and interesting as there are other issues involved such as nationality, race, culture, choice of country to live in and basic communication.

MATCHMAKING

In older generations, many marriages were arranged by a matchmaking agency. The parents and matchmaker would try to find a suitable mate for their child. Parents and children would meet or have lunch together to see if the two prospective marriage partners liked each other.

In modern times, this arrangement is not as popular. Many young people want to find their own soul mate. Sometimes however, parents try to find a suitable match for their child by themselves through friends and co-workers and may casually make an introduction over lunch.

There are also matchmaking agencies for international couples. Singles who want to meet someone are matched up for a fee.

WEDDINGS

It is not unusual for couples to get legally married by signing the documents and having the wedding ceremony the next year. Whenever I go to the American Embassy in Tokyo, I always see many couples, invariably American men and Japanese women obtaining documents to get married. The wedding ceremony may be Japanese style or Western style.

In western style weddings, which are popular and big business nowadays, the ceremony is held in a structure that looks like a church. Some hotels even have their own chapel. A tuxedo and gown is worn and the ceremony may not even be performed by a real priest. He might be any westerner who matches their image as a priest. This part-time 'minister' might be somebody with a full-time job.

The reception dinner is usually held in a hotel and consists of very expensive food. Guests usually give cash as a gifts which averages around $300. Relatives usually give more.

GOOD POINTS

In a survey of some Westerners and Japanese in Japan, most of those surveyed believed, not surprisingly that Western men and women, and Japanese men and women living in Japan were very different. How are they different? People who were surveyed said that the following are some good points of certain men and women in Japan. People who were surveyed said that:

Some Japanese Women were perceived to be:
- Feminine, receptive, cheerful
- Fashionable, pretty, healthy diet
- Deferential to men
- Shy, in appearance or in fact
- Have a Favorable image historically

Some Western Women were perceived to be:
- Pretty, consider non-materialistic values
- Educated , native English speaker
- Foreign, different, rarity

- From affluent, interesting, admired country
- Independent, strong, career-oriented

Some Japanese Men were perceived to be:
- Hard-working, team-oriented
- Educated, skilled
- Have a Calm demeanor
- Gives salary to wife to control
- Familiar with Japan

Some Western Men were perceived to be:
- Confident, individualistic, liberal
- Educated, native English speaker
- Foreign, different, rarity
- From affluent, interesting, admired country
- Chivalrous, shares housework, supports family

DATING PERCENTAGES OF WESTERNERS

Let's look at some dating percentages from a sample of Westerners in Japan.

Total Female and Male Westerners Sampled
Females   39%

Males	61%
Total	100%

Females Westerners
Females with Western Boyfriends	45%
Females not dating	45%
Females with Japanese Boyfriends	10%
Total	100%

Males Westerners
Males with Japanese Girlfriends	50%
Males not dating	15%
Males with Japanese Wives	14%
Males with Western Girlfriends	14%
Males with Western Wives	7%
Total	100%

Total Female and Male Westerners
Western Men with Japanese Girlfriends	30%
Not dating	27%
Western Women with Western Boyfriends	17%
Western Men married to Japanese Women	9%
Western Men with Western Girlfriends	9%
Western Men with Western Wives	4%

Western Women with Japanese Boyfriends 4%
Total   100%

SUMMARY

If the supposition is true that the perception of ordinary western men suddenly changes to extraordinary men when they arrive in Japan and are able to easily woo beauty-queen level Japanese women, (although the attractiveness gap is sometimes exaggerated and narrower than we joke about), then either these western men are socially shrewd or just really lucky to have found themselves in a favorable male-market, regular-guy –friendly social situation.

I think many of my extraordinary fellow male Westerners are attractive to women but what do I know I'm a guy. And besides guys don't really look at each other when we are talking, we just kind of talk in the other guys direction. As for myself, I am ordinary. I straddle the line between geekness and cooldom and haven't been indicted for being attractive, at least not since last century sometime, I can't remember exactly. But I hope that personal attributes such as selflessness, generosity, good manners, kindness, honesty, humor and common sense will make the ultimate difference in a relationship. GET OUTTA HERE!... No, really, really.

PART II

2

AN AUGUST DAY

'WHAT'S THAT %#&@ NOISE?' screamed someone in a low, intimidating, heavily accented voice at 3 o'clock in the morning. Although these irate blasts trespassed through the flimsy walls dividing my room and the hallway-kitchen, they were not directed at me. The terrible twosome of street hawkers had just returned from their night jobs and they were partying in the tiny hallway, and the disturbed houseguest was just saying what I, writhing on my futon bedding, was thinking.

A travel book had listed this foreigner guesthouse and I didn't know what to expect. The structure was old, small and expensive but conveniently located in central Tokyo. My eyes now clearly open, I felt insecure as it was my first night in Japan, and I hadn't seen the faces so I couldn't match them to the voices. One could only imagine. It didn't help matters that my door lock was broken and the only thing keeping it closed was the white, electrical cord of my portable fan that was loosely wrapped around the doorknob. Then ...

That was several summers ago. This summer's day developed less dramatically.

August A.M. Greater Tokyo Area

    Sabers of sunlight stabbed through the slit between my drawn curtains as time drew sights in on 10:30, and the giant cicadas squeaked incessantly in symphony with the sibilant sounds of the songbirds. The eyelid of my strong eye gradually slid open before the weaker one, and I negotiated myself off my cushy, floored futon and into the unit bathroom. The morning was late but I was not tardy, and I gave thanks because I remember the early workdays when I had to spit on six.
    As I forked my breakfast of steamed rice, fried eggs and cold grapefruit into my mouthhole, I absorbed the American Forces Network radio program and glanced at a culinary program on TV. After breakfast, I donned my teacher's uniform of long sleeved shirt, solid pants and conservative tie, and shouldered my worn, black backpack containing a plastic bagged lunch and my constant companion, an

omnipotent, all seeing, all-knowing, soon-to-be-obsolete, camera, internet cell phone.

Don't things seem to go in a full circle? During my elementary school days, I was required to wear khaki pants and a white shirt. It was very plain but economical, and usual for a Catholic, parochial uniform in Honolulu. Today I am wearing khaki pants and a white dress shirt (it is fashionable again) as I head to school as a teacher. Another image comes to mind; a tie, a backpack and a bicycle remind me of an image of some missionaries' clothes, except we don't preach religion we preach grammar.

Shoes must be left in a square, sunken space inside the apartment in front of the door. I slide them on. My apartment is a studio with a tiny loft, a desk, a midget fridge, a TV, a VCR, a wooden floor, white walls and a narrow balcony- not nicely appointed but functional. My bicycle looks like it is from the 1950s as my friend says, but they all look like this. I mount and ride.

Around a tight corner, I bolt like lightning and down the street, I cruise like the wind, yet a mother with two kids on her bike passes me as I splice through some sweet potato and corn farms. Now these farms are not what you might imagine, as the size of them is the same as that of an American backyard or any billionaire's kitchen.

As I ride, kernels of sweat form on my forehead in reaction to the summer heat. Then greenery and houses give way to rare sidewalked streets, cute boxy cars and camel-hump-seat buses (passengers seated over the protruding tire casing must endure their knees pressing against the chests). Dark glasses protect my eyes from the sun and swirling dust, yet people always stare at me as only juvenile ruffians and punch-permed, four-fingered henchmen wear them.

The street climbs a bit until the uniform, auto-door taxis and their once retired drivers smoking or swinging a golf club appear, and then the bus rotary, with patient, queuing locals, show up and here - covered, concrete, decorated with green trim, movie advertisements and amorous pigeons is - the local train station.

I lock my rusty bicycle with the other thousand or so bikes that encircle the station like an iron and rubber lei. The video store, open-air sushi shop, gambler-filled pachinko shop, American-type donut shop, Japanese bread shop, part-time ATM (closed nights and weekends), convenience store and police station that serve this station town have opened for business.

I insert my monthly train pass in the station gate and wait for the train that always comes on time, except when there is a 'human body accident'. One year ago, I was riding in the first car of the train as it rolled into the station. Then suddenly, the horn filled our eardrums and we screeched to an awkward stop. A poor soul had jumped onto the track (it is not so rare) and we had to wait like train passengers turned train prisoners inside the compartment as train workers accounted for the body parts. Unwittingly, I spied between a group of green uniformed maintenance workers huddling near the track and I saw a pair of panted legs, still as death itself, with pea-green faded socks on shoeless feet.

As usual, today's train is exactly on time. Because of the off-peak hour, the train is not busy and I can sit down. There are a lot of solitary housewives, sleepy students, and a smattering of suited salarymen. Seats are cushioned bench style and space is never in surplus, yet a few males sit with their legs open wider than cooked clamshells on a bed of pasta taking up space for two. The compartment is cool and there are advertisements on the wall and hanging from the ceiling usually showing pictures of news, tea, cell phones, beer, schools, electrical appliances or busty girls in undersized swimsuits.

My turf is the outlying Tokyo suburb near the surf of north Tokyo Bay, in the eastern part of the Los Angeles-like Tokyo Metropolitan expanse. And like LA, Tokyo proper is not so big yet the greater Tokyo area is one contiguous mass of buildings, infrastructure and houses that extend well into the adjoining prefectures. Everyone refers to the entire area as 'To-kyo' (two syllables). New Tokyo Narita Airport is about an hour away by train, as is Tokyo Disneyland and Disneysea and the Imperial Palace.

The six stops to my school take three minutes per stop. So after a short eighteen minutes, I step on to the elevated platform and start dodging the never-ending mishmash of traipsing or scurrying people.

This is the station where centuries ago, samurai crossed the river on a bridge of adjacent ships. This is where train tracks still snake - a legacy to confuse bombers during World War II. This is where an old-timer tells of American bombers dropping their last bombs after unloading on Tokyo. This is where not one but two horse racetracks operate. This is the town where locals could once smell the salty scent of Tokyo Bay before miles of ocean were reclaimed and paved. And this is where the military communication center was once located, which sent the secret code 'Climb Mount Nitaka,' signaling gunships to rendezvous for the attack on Pearl Harbor during WWII.

At my school, I teach several classes a day. Our goal is to help students improve their conversational English for travelling, work or simply as a hobby.

After 8 hours, school is out. At 9:00 PM, I clock and rock and I am on the train by 9:10. The train is jammed with salarymen and office ladies and smells of alcohol. In the train stations there are random patches of sand covering the 'platform pizza' regurgitated by soused employees.

Near my station, there is a supermarket that is open 24 hours and I buy some food to cook for dinner. Today, I buy boneless chicken thighs, white peaches and orange juice. Teriyaki chicken cooks easily and, keeping the food pyramid in mind, I balance the marinated fowl with some fresh steamed spinach and rice. As I sit on the floor in a folded-legged pose and dine off my foot high table, I focus on the translated, stop-and-go-flow bilingual news.

Before entering the prefabricated bathroom to take a shower, I adjust the water temperature setting on the wall. The muggy summer's day has taken its toll, and the sprouts of showering liquid feel like a religious experience.

Being far from the station allows the nights around my second floor apartment to be still, and quiet enough to hear the crickets. A cool wet wind, not gusty, violent or intrusive, sifts through my sliding screen door from Tokyo Bay, which sleeps two miles from here. Around 1:00AM, I ease onto my futon to get some REM shuteye and drift off into the welcoming night.

3

Q&A

What kind of Education Do I Need?

Americans need a four year degree (any major) to get a working Visa. Citizens from other countries may not need a degree. For example, young Australians and Canadians can get a working holiday visa without a degree. If you apply for a visa in Japan, you must present your ORIGINAL Diploma to immigration. Bring the original in its folder and not a copy.

Schools are not concerned about the type of degree. They want a native English speaker and they assume that University graduates have this basic ability therefore a degree in teaching or English in not necessary. A degree in physics, business, anthropology, art or anything else has been acceptable.

Do I need experience?

No experience is needed. Schools hire inexperienced native English speakers. New teachers can quickly learn teaching techniques through training and start teaching immediately.

Some teachers have just finished their University degree while others have worked at other jobs that were not related to teaching. There have been former salespeople, restaurant workers, dishwashers, miners, coaches, navy personnel and hotel staff. A small minority has had teaching experience.

Some great teachers have a background in teaching yet some of the best teachers haven't had any experience. The best teachers can adapt to the teaching style and understand the needs of Japanese students. They are also friendly, are able to explain well and make learning enjoyable.

Do I have to speak Japanese?

No Japanese is needed. All teaching is done using 100% English. Most students have at least 6 years of English schooling and can read and write. They are weak at speaking because they haven't had an opportunity to practice so they need to speak to a native English speaker.

Like any other skill, one must practice to improve and the more the students listen and speak English the better they will become.

At certain schools, if Japanese is used as part of the teaching process, a Japanese teacher will assist the English teacher with Japanese. But the English teacher does not need to speak Japanese.

Is Japan expensive?

Not unreasonably. It compares equally to large American cities and currently Japan is experiencing deflation. Salary is commensurate with the cost of living and taxes are low. After we live here for a while, we know where to find markets, shops and restaurants that have reasonable or cheap prices. We can save money if we don't spend excessively.

REASONABLE	EXPENSIVE
Market food	Restaurants
Household goods	Travel, Transportation, Telephone
Clothes	Movies
Taxes	Drinking

Note:
1) There are many 100-yen stores where we can buy many cheap products including household goods and thousands of other products. These are comparable to the $1.00 stores back home. Once we enter

these shops, it is almost impossible to leave without wanting to buy something.
2) We have to pay national income tax, city tax and consumption (sales) tax, which right now is 5 %. Some taxes are user-based taxes such as highway tolls. Drivers using the highway must pay a hefty fee as they exit. It is not a 'free'way. The good point is that if we don't drive (most teachers don't), then we don't have to pay this tax.

Can I get a job?

English is immensely popular and schools hire throughout the year. There are many schools in the large metropolitan areas and if we keep looking the opportunity may come. Teachers come and go every month so there are always job openings. Be aware that there is competition for jobs.

It is not difficult to get an interview. Getting hired depends on the interview process and therefore it is a good idea to prepare for this step. The school will hire based on the interview. They want a friendly candidate that students will like.

What are the good and bad points of being an English Teacher?

GOOD POINTS	BAD POINTS
Easy to teach/learn curriculum	Misunderstanding

Meeting people	Repeating oneself often
Short Hours	Talking all day
Easygoing Atmosphere	Very slow speaking pace
Friendly Teachers/Students	Must smile all day
Comfortable School setting	Microteaching

<u>Be an English Teacher Test</u>

- ❑ Do you like meeting people?
- ❑ Do you like talking and listening?
- ❑ Do you enjoy teaching?
- ❑ Do you like taking to people who speak in varying degrees of non-fluent English?
- ❑ Do you like time-based work rather than a project-oriented work?

Note: If most of your answers are 'Yes", you would enjoy being an English teacher.

What makes a good teacher?

A good teacher should be friendly, competent, patient, and humorous. Additionally, a good English teacher will know when to listen and when to talk. A lecturer will speak for one hour but a language a teacher will try to encourage students to speak as much as possible. The more the students speak the better they become. The teacher should listen for two things: the students' concerns and the students' mistakes. Finally, the teacher should give positive feedback on the mistakes, recommend correction, make suggestions and give encouragement.

What kind of person would like living and working in Japan?

The people that have enjoyed living here seem to like teaching, have Japanese and Western friends, and have many interests such as travelling or studying culture and language. They enjoy the different culture and can assimilate well.

Many of the teachers enjoy travelling often to different places. They focus on the good points of living in another country and aren't fazed by the frustrating ones. The person is also independent and can do things on their own whenever necessary. They may be adventurous as well because they are so many new things to see and do. Working in Japan is not just a job, it is a life.

<u>Live in Japan Test</u>

- Do you like to travel?
- Do you like different people, different things and a different way of life?

- Are you independent?
- Do you enjoy change?
- Are you flexible?

Note: If 'Yes', then you would enjoy living in Japan.

What kind of person leaves soon?

A few Westerners leave after days, weeks or months. Some want to travel. Others become homesick and miss their family. Some Westerners can't get used to the many differences here. They expect things to be the same as back home.

Leave soon Test

- Do you get homesick easily?
- Do you need familiar surroundings?
- Do you dislike crowds?
- Do you dislike travelling?
- Do you need a Western lifestyle (food, gender-treatment, etc.)?

Note: If 'Yes', you may leave soon. But if your contract has an early termination clause, there is no problem. It doesn't mean that your stay wasn't a success or enjoyable. It just was for a short time. Most people don't stay forever anyway.

Should I apply from the U.S. or apply in Japan?

1) First, check the Internet for ESL schools and organizations that interview and hire in the U.S. (Search: 'Teaching English in Japan'. It has the most hits). They may have a recruiting branch in the U.S., Canada, Australia, England and other English-speaking countries. Some schools take recruiting trips to various cities. You may have to fly to a major city for an interview if they don't come to your town.

2) If you can't find a job from the U.S. and really want to work in Japan, go ahead and fly to Japan. Schools will know you are serious and will hire someone they can interview in person. You will be able to apply at many more companies and schools that have job openings. There are a lot companies and smaller schools that need teachers. BE AWARE that obtaining a job and visa in Japan is competitive and not easy. There are no guarantees that you can get a job or visa. At any given time, there is a community of ESL job seekers and you will see them during the interview process. They are your competition but because they, like us are all English speakers with a similar goal in a foreign country, can be our new friends. During the job search, let me say again that

there are no guarantees but interviews are not hard to get and one more step from the interview is getting hired.

What kind of applicant will the school hire?

Let's think back when we were in school or at the University. What kind of teacher did we like? We liked someone who was friendly, interesting, funny and smart. We liked a professor that was easy to understand and answered our questions. We enjoyed a good laugh and became enthralled with intriguing topics that were well presented.

Basically, there are two kinds of English students; the serious student and the recreational student. Both kinds of students are equally important to the school. The serious student wants a smart teacher and the recreational student wants an interesting and funny teacher. Both of them want a friendly teacher.

Some job interviews have written or verbal tests. Some tests are on grammar or vocabulary. Some schools want to look at University transcripts. Others interviews require impromptu lessons while most require only dialog.

In summary, schools are looking for someone who is:
- Friendly
- Interesting
- Funny
- Smart

It may be hard to demonstrate all of these attributes in an interview so being friendly is the most important.

Tell me more about the students.

In Japan, students range from 2 to 80 years old. Most children from 2 to 12 are learning English because their parents want them to. For some of them, it is the first time to use English or meet a foreigner. Some of them would rather be outside playing while most of them enjoy the lesson.

Many students from 13 to 18 already have ambitions and want to learn English. They are intelligent and have the best pronunciation because they started early.

Many University students want to study English for future careers.

Most adults study for their work as they have jobs that require some English. Many of them study for travel. Housewives study for travel or as a hobby. Many of my private students are housewives.

Middle age and Senior citizens study for various reasons. Some of them are fluent because they have been studying for years and have the highest knowledge of vocabulary.

Jobs

A majority of them are office people – 'salarymen' and 'office ladies' as they refer to themselves. This includes many types of engineers such as system engineers, sales engineers or computer engineers. There are pilots, travel agents, cabin attendants, doctors, nurses, pharmacists, teachers, salespeople, part-time workers and many more. Some don't have jobs.

A few of them are electrical linemen, forklift operators or carpenters. They are 'blue collar' students in what is often thought of as a 'white collar' world of English study. English study welcomes everyone. They seem to prosper in school and I really enjoy teaching them, as I am kind of a blue-collar guy in my own way.

Several students work for well-known American or foreign companies. Many of them work for famous Japanese conglomerates.

Time of Day

Generally speaking, during the day students, retirees and housewives take lessons. At night and on the weekend, the salaried workers come to study.

Gender

There is generally even split between men and women but it depends on the location. Suburban areas have an even mix and business areas have many businessmen. Among the high schoolers and the elderly, there seem to be many females. Many businessmen study for their work.

Do I need a Visa?

U.S. citizens are given a reciprocal visa exemption that allows a stay for three months without a visa. You may enter Japan without a visa if you have a U.S. passport. At Japanese immigration, they will stamp an entry date in your passport and you can stay for three months from that date. Other countries given this exemption are Argentina, Belgium, Denmark, Finland, France, Iceland, Malaysia, Netherlands, Singapore, Canada, Israel, New Zealand, Italy, Norway, Spain, Sweden and a few more. The UK, Austria, Germany, Ireland, Mexico and Switzerland are exempt for six months. These visas are for those who are not planning to work.

Working Holiday visas are granted to Australians, Canadians and New Zealanders. The visa time limit is for a maximum of eighteen months and allows young people under 30 to work and travel.

Americans need a Working Visa to work in Japan. If you are hired in the States, the company can help you get it. If you are hired in Japan, you must leave Japan to obtain the visa at a Japanese Embassy in another country then reenter Japan to work. Generally working visas are granted for one or three years.

PART III

4

A JOB HUNTING STORY

Obviously, it is much easier if one can secure a job before coming to Japan as that ensures that one has a place to stay, salary, peace of mind and it allows one to focus on a definite plan. I recommend looking for a job over the Internet (the easiest way), Japanese embassy or a school that has an American-based office and try to sign a contract before coming to Japan. I tried to apply to in this manner but the competitive job market in Hawaii prevented me from being hired.

However, since I was determined to work in Japan, I did it the challenging way. Without a job, work visa, place to stay, language ability or friends, I got on the plane and came to Tokyo. A few days before I left, I had second thoughts- "I'm leaving a comfortable lifestyle, friends, family, my much-loved convertible RX-7 with headrest stereo speakers (sob) and a place I love." Leaving Honolulu for a long time is never easy. From the airport departure lounge, the view of Diamond Head against the blue late morning sky looks three times better than the best postcard, bright, clear and breathtaking. It is overwhelming evidence that the Hawaii State motto rings true: 'Ua mau ke ea o ka aina I ka pono' (The life of the land is perpetuated in righteousness).

Nine hours later, the plane set down in the land of the legendary samurai. After disembarking at Narita Airport, I had to ask someone how to use the strange-looking public phone in order to call the foreigner guesthouse. I rode the rapid train for two hours and arrived in western Tokyo. At the station, I was met by a slim, forty-something Japanese man who spoke haphazard English. He led me through a mini-maze of tight streets and lanes around a neighborhood bustling with low-ceiling shops, self-barbecue restaurants and speeding pedestrians. Distance is defined by minutes on foot rather than measure of length as streets and blocks are irregular and often incomprehensible.

Sixteen minutes later we arrived at an old house and as we entered, I couldn't help but inhale the stench of shoes siting at the front entrance. The guesthouse was a wooden house converted to a 2-story rooming house with 4 rooms and kitchen upstairs and 4 rooms, a toilet and a shower downstairs. The word room is an overstatement, they were more like unfurnished, unpainted bar-less detention cells. My first reaction was one of disbelief. I couldn't believe that people lived like this. But the weathered house was full, rent was reasonable, and it was located in central Tokyo. Besides, what better option did I have?

My upstairs room had a Japanese TV, a tattered futon, a much-used blanket, a briefcase-sized window and a fan. It was June and the thick air was humid but not yet oppressive. On this Trans-Pacific excursion of the non-routine kind, a few good, bad and unforgettable things happened.

A long mop-haired, artist-wanna-be, 50-something Swedish man painted in the next room. He had two Japanese girlfriends who came on alternating nights. Although not perturbed he always yelled and spat when he talked. Downstairs lived a soft-spoken, blond dreadlocked gentleman from New Zealand who played 70's rock music on the street for a living and walked around paved Tokyo barefooted. He said he played on different city streets around the world.

In another a room, two Mediterranean men lived, one a street vendor of rings and bracelets, and the other a juggler for coins. They hustled their wares and services for street donations in aggressive, people-packed Shibuya. A gay couple, a Canadian English teacher and his Japanese boyfriend occupied the corner room. The dedicated boyfriend daintily prepared savory gourmet dinners in the common kitchen, while the teacher was at work. Everyone was in Tokyo for work or travel, and communicated in borderline-fluent, accented English.

Believing that Japan was a safe country, I left my new brown leather-hiking boots at the front door, which is customary here, but they were stolen one week later.

On my first night there, I noticed that my door lock didn't work, so I tied the off-white, portable fan cord around the doorknob to secure the flimsy door. At about 3:00 A.M., the street vendor and juggler tumbled into the weak-walled, noise-intolerant house, and proceeded to make merriment in the kitchen and hallway. The party continued for twenty minutes when suddenly the Swede gangbusted out from his room into the common area and started to lambaste the two in a rant that lasted for 5 long minutes and tested the limits of his formidable lungs. No argument. No worries. Quiet. The uncontested Swede crawled back into his hole.

Five minutes of silence passed and ended when the party started again as loud as ever, as if nothing had just happened. Unbelievable! Abomination! No one protested this time and the dancing, prancing, talking and drinking lasted for an hour. At 4:00 A.M., the oblivious party punks went to sleep and finally, so could I.

The refrigerator germinated dark, fuzzy organisms that had once been recognizable food. A Japanese toilet was there to be used and using it was never a cinch. Only the brave, dexterous or indigested dare try. I often sought refuge at an American fast food restaurant, which had western toilets. There was an auto-pay shower with a semi-transparent door near the front entrance, so lodgers couldn't be shy if we wanted to keep clean. The shower cost 50 yen for 5 minutes, which meant that our timing had to be perfect especially when soap was on our face or shampoo was in our hair.

Next to the rooming house was a vegetable store where the owner's daughter was able to speak English. I won't forget the kind owner of a corner grocery market who didn't charge me tax, as he knew I was a foreigner and must have thought that I was strapped for money.

On Monday morning I bought English newspaper and scanned the employment section for English Teaching positions. I called many schools and went to countless interviews over a three-month period. Americans have an automatic visa exemption for a three-month period as tourists and the starting date is the date stamped on our passport as we enter Japan. We must leave within three months or violate immigration law. My goal was to sign a contract and apply for a working visa with a school's sponsorship while in Japan. Then after receiving an approval card from Japan's immigration office in the mail I would have to obtain my working visa in another country, preferably in my home country on a specified date then reenter Japan on an official working visa to begin teaching.

While this may sound convoluted and troublesome, many teachers have done it. Worthwhile goals require persistence and action. They say lucky and accomplished people work hard to meet their goals. While I was interviewing, a whole community of other job seekers looking for teaching jobs pounded the paved streets of this eastern jungle.

One memorable interview took me to Matsumoto City, north of Tokyo. From Tokyo station, I rode a train, to be specific between train cars, with several other passengers, standing for two hours in a cramped, claustrophobic, no-mans-land. As seats became vacant further from the city center, I was able to go into the regular train car and finally rest my pin and needle legs.

In Matsumoto, I visited a wooden castle that had a hidden floor designed to hide retreating royalty from warring invaders, and saw a dried monkey head sitting sadly in a window of an odd medicine shop. My 'interview' was preceded by five minutes of panicky preparation for an impromptu lesson for two real students.

At other schools, I was served cold tea or responded to questions in group interviews. Sometimes candidates were reimbursed for expensive train fare or paid good money for taking a written test. At other times, many applicants were ignored like stale fish bait in a school of pompous fish as the school owner serenaded the prototype candidate.

I was able to engage some private students through a Teacher-Student-matching agency, and taught them over coffee in a donut shop. This was not difficult to do, as there was a shortage of English Teachers relative to the demand.

Teachers can't live by privates alone so trying another approach, I listed my name in the free classified magazine under jobs wanted. A teacher from Arizona called me and asked me to replace him for two weeks while he was away on vacation. During this period, I experienced teaching in a classroom setting for the first time and tried to pick up some simple teaching techniques. Being native English speakers, we already have the basic knowledge of pronunciation, grammar and expressions. Teaching English is just a matter of learning some basic teaching methods and getting to know the students strong and weak points.

Basically, to teach in Japan, Americans need a four-year Bachelors Degree in any subject. Japan, with its own agenda, prefers that only certain foreigners live in its country.

In 1854, American Matthew Perry opened a reclusive Japan. However, in modern times it is barely open. There is 'free' trade yet as evidenced by the U.S.-Japan trade deficit Japan would rather sell than buy. Only 1% of the population is foreign and compared to other developed nations this country accepts a very small amount of refugees. Nippon has never been colonized, has been secluded either geographically or politically for much of its history and enforces a strict immigration policy. Hence, it has a homogenous population.

It has labored hard and built itself to be economically successful, safe and culturally rich. To continue this prosperity, it currently believes that a restrictive immigration policy is a key part of the larger plan and will expediently accept, in general, educated skilled foreigners who can help the country or teach its citizens. And Japan, like all countries does what it believes is best to protect itself and its citizens.

The job hunting competition took me in its toll and after nearly 3 months, I had earned some money, met many people, drank, ate and gone sightseeing, but I had not signed a contract or obtained a visa. So, on a rainy day in August, having ambivalent feelings but no alternatives, I returned to my islands waiting in the middle of the sea.

In balmy Honolulu, my decision was already set – to not look for a full-time job at home as I was determined to come back to Japan and try again. I studied Japanese at the community center at night and returned to Tokyo in May. Americans and certain foreigners are able to enter Nippon multiple times with a 3-month visa exemption, which automatically renews itself when we leave the country. Then we can enter Japan again for three more months. But we can't do it too often, as our intentions will be questioned.

Back at the same Tokyo auslander house, I met some pretty Australian hostesses, some South Korean travelers (one of them gave me a pack of cigarettes as a gesture of friendship), and some girls from Hong Kong. There was also a half-German, half-Japanese girl from Canada who said she couldn't sleep well because her body was longer than her miniscule room under the stairs.

I started to look at the employment ads again and found a school that offered me a job. I returned to Honolulu to pick up that precious visa sticker, and entered Japan officially on a working visa. Plans change and so did mine as I had intended to stay for only a year but have not left yet.

Time seems to move fast here. I've lived in five different apartments, said goodbye to a number of friends, and seen teachers and students come and go – needless to say, I've changed. Most teachers sign a contract before they come to Japan and already have a job and an apartment waiting for them upon arrival. Yet I heard one of these teachers complain that he had to wait at the Narita airport for 1 hour before the teacher escort picked him up. When I first arrived at Narita airport, I didn't have a house, a job, a visa, any friends or any language skills. Anyway, after some tears, fears and cheers, I am able to appreciate what I have.

5

STEP 1

THE BIG DECISION

T he decision to work in Japan loomed large for me because:

- I had a good life in Honolulu and no clear well-defined one in Japan. It wasn't a lifelong dream from my childhood to work in Japan. Life is dynamic and it wasn't until recently that I became interested in coming here.
- My major was accounting, not Japanese. I had registered for Japanese at the University but later dropped the class because language didn't suit me. The Business College at the University of Hawaii didn't require language. Being a jack of a few trades and

master of none, I worked as a CPA and a computer programmer. I was not an English Teacher.

- I was not forced to go and there was no urgency to go. In a way having less options makes things easier because it takes away the excruciating process of life changing decision-making. The fork in the road soon disappears after we pass through it and once we make a decision we can't go back. Just before I left Honolulu, I told my brother I was feeling very apprehensive. A few years later, I think it was one of the best decisions in my life.

Just meeting people, eating good food, seeing and learning about another world is fascinating and I came to Japan because I wanted to come and the time was right for me. Furthermore, I negotiated with myself. I thought that I would stay here for one year and then return so I didn't sell my car and kept my life in Honolulu on hold and I felt comfortable with this. We have to decide for ourselves and there are a few ways we can do it.

- Do it fast. Do it now.
- Write down the good and bad points and make a logical decision.
- We should get to know ourselves. It might be right for us now or ten years from now. Only we know about our own feelings as reality and happiness are in our minds and often a matter of timing.

- ❏ Compromise with our life and ourselves. Try it for 1 year or take a trip to check it out.
- ❏ Talk to our friends and family. They can be the Board of Directors of our life and we are the Chairman of the Board.

If we are willing to be open to new things and customs and people and like to travel then it is probably right for us. If we are set in our ways and need only familiar surroundings then maybe it is not. Keep in mind that actions here may be done inexplicably and senselessly and we can't expect them to make sense in our world. On the other hand, things may appear rational and we may wonder why we don't do it that way in our world.

6

STEP 2

PACK LIGHT PLAN WELL

WHERE- The best place to job hunt is in the metropolitan area such as Tokyo or Osaka because there are many schools, companies and jobs. Rural areas recruit from the large cities. Large schools hire in the city and may send teachers to rural areas. Go to the large urban cities.

WHEN-Schools hire year-round. The school and business year starts in April so there are many job openings in February and March.

PACK:

1. **ORIGINAL Diploma- Bachelors Degree . You cannot present a copy to immigration.**

2. Suit and tie. Skirt and jacket
3. Passport
4. Money
5. Resume
6. Warm clothes - if you come during winter (generally it will be cold or cool from November to April and it depends on the area)
7. Good socks or stockings as some organizations require that shoes be removed
8. Everything else can be bought here although they may not be exactly like those at home

Conservative Budget for 1 Month

1. Airfare $1000
2. Rooming house $500
3. Food $300
4. Miscellaneous $200
Total $2000

Note:
1) This is just an estimate. You may spend less and have money left over. If you find a job soon, your salary will sustain you. Japan is not cheap therefore salaries are not low. If you

go to a less developed country, your salary would be lower. You can earn this 'investment' back in several months.

2) **Carry your passport and money with you all the time.** From my experience, it seems that the rooming houses are not that safe and foreigners are always required to carry identification.

7

STEP 3

MAKE 2 RESERVATIONS AND SOAR TO THIS LAND

Look on the Internet for reasonable fare and make an airline reservation. Many American, Australian, British, Canadian, Japanese and Asian airlines fly to Japan. Look at it as a short vacation that may bring some great opportunities.

On the Internet or a book on Japan, you can find a foreign guesthouse. If you don't like it you can always move to another one. These houses are cheaper than hotels and for foreigners, it is impossible to meet the requirements for an apartment contract. These houses give you an opportunity to meet new friends, maybe some teachers who can provide some useful job information. Some houses are much better than others are. It depends on the location, facilities, residents and price. Call them from your home country and make a reservation before you arrive. Have a backup guesthouse in mind just in case the first one doesn't work out.

8

STEP 4

ON MONDAY BUY THE ENGLISH NEWSPAPER

For the fisherman at sea who has the right bait, who is in the right location and who cast out many lines, the odds for landing the big tuna become more favorable. So for the job hunter on land, dress professionally, search in the large city and call all the schools that seem interesting and go to every possible interview. During this time you can increase your understanding of the interview process and English schools' needs.

BEFORE THE INTERVIEW

1. Dress neatly in a suit and tie or skirt and jacket.

2. Obtain detailed directions as streets are complicated.

Example of directions to a school heard over the phone:

Get on the Minami subway until you arrive at Nishibashi station. Transfer to the Kita train line at platform 1. Get off at bashi station use the main gate and turn right. You will see a police station then turn left. Walk along the street for 2 minutes, cross over the Higashi train tracks and after 1 minute you will see a drugstore on your left. Turn left down the small lane and walk for 3 minutes. When you get to the street you will see a 5-story building go to the 3rd floor.

Write down all directions as streets and addresses are not clearly shown.

3. Go early. Allow for train delays. It is easy to get lost.

DURING THE INTERVIEW

DO
1. Smile and be friendly (schools want friendly teachers)
2. Ask some questions. For example:
    a. What are my duties?

b. Will I be trained?
c. What teaching materials will I use?
d. What is the teaching process?
e. Who are the students?
f. Where will I live?
g. What are the terms of the contract? Resignation clause? hours?
3. Show your motivation, explain how you can help the school and state clearly that you would like to work there
4. Listen and be attentive

DON'T
1. Act like an expert and talk excessively
2. Give one work answers
3. Appear bored
4. Don't ask about the salary, they will tell you.

AFTER THE INTERVIEW

1. Follow up with a letter or phone call to show interest.
2. Continue to look for a job.

The job hunter can't control such factors as interviewer preconceived images and we can't alter our personal profile.

Consequently we need to focus on the controllable factors (clothes and interview) that will make or break one's progress towards successfully obtaining a job. Innate intelligence if always handy yet not enough as an English Teacher is also a salesperson, motivator, friend, actor, diplomat, communicator, mind-reader, cultural ambassador and often an entertainer.

Schools want instructors who can:
1. sell their product to potential students through demonstration lessons
2. effectively instruct grammar, vocabulary, listening comprehension, pronunciation and idioms
3. Retain current students by keeping them interested and motivated
4. Relate well with students and management
5. Be reliable and professional

Without cluttering your head too much, **just smile, be friendly, and enjoy yourself.**

Other sources to look for a job are:

1. Free English publications at large English bookstores.
2. Community papers and bulletin boards.

3. Talk to other foreigners and teachers in the rooming house or foreign hangouts such as Roppongi, Azabu, Omontesando and stations along the Yamanote Line.
4. Surf the Internet for openings (Key words: 'Teaching English in Japan' (most hits), ESL, Japan, English, Teaching).

9

STEP 5

IF WE PERSIST, THE OFFER WILL COME

Continue to call schools and go to interviews. Have fun. Enjoy the atmosphere around the stations and towns near the school and take side trips to famous temples and castles. Savor the cuisine and drink in a Japanese Izakaya (bar). Socialize with the locals. They are friendly and want to meet English-speaking foreigners.

Most schools offer a one-year contract for a full-time job of 30-40 hours a week including 2 weeks of vacation. The contract pays at least 250,000 yen ($2500) a month as this is the amount required to qualify for a visa. As with any legal document, it is recommended that you understand the terms well. Some schools allow teachers to terminate the contract anytime with only a 30-day notice.

After an applicant signs the contract, the school will help with the visa application. Wait for the approval letter, which will tell you when, and where to pick it up. It is necessary to fly to another country outside Japan preferably our home country and obtain the visa from the Japanese embassy on the specified date. Then you can return to Japan officially on a working visa. It takes time, effort and money, however the money can be recouped in several months and the time is spent travelling and learning.

During the interview process at one school, I had to take a difficult written English Test. In another school, I took a written test and was paid well for it. And another required an impromptu lesson to real students as the owner observed. Many of them just required talking. The following may help you in an interview or if you have to teach an impromptu lesson.

STUDENTS STRONG POINTS

- Six requisite years of English
- Can read and write basic words
- Use some basic English words in their language
- Respect teachers
- Friendly, smiling, agreeable, modest and teachable

STUDENT WEAK POINTS

- Beginners are quiet, shy and hesitate to initiate conversation (of course it depends on the individual. Many students are very outgoing)
- Afraid to make mistakes
- Japanese language has flat intonation
- Pronunciation doesn't have 'r' 'th' 'v' sounds (rain='lain')
- Japanese language sentence structure. subject+object+verb ('I market to the went ')

COMMON MISTAKES
- 'I go to shopping'
- 'I play ski'
- 'I back home'
- 'It has many nature'
- 'Yesterday I go to work'

SOME GRAMMAR POINTS
- Present perfect - I have eaten
- Tag questions – It is sunny, isn't it?
- Unreal if – If I were rich, I would buy a boat.
- Passive voice - It is made in the USA.
- Reported speech – He said he had eaten it.

IMPROMPTU LESSON PLAN (10minutes)

- Name Introductions
- Write and explain lesson's function or grammar point
- Practice with examples
- Help pronunciation and vocabulary
- Role play real situation
- Give correction, suggestions, positive reinforcement

Below is corresponding example

IMPROMPTU LESSON EXAMPLE(1 or 2 minutes a step)
- My name is …(and make a joke to break the ice)…
- 'Today's lesson is past tense -I went to the beach'…
- 'I went to the market' 'I ate pizza' ' I bought shoes'…
- 'carrot' not callot'…
- 'Let's do a role play about -Two friends talking about yesterday…'
- Not 'I eated' 'I ate' 'For yesterday always use past tense' 'Excellent Akiko!

Knowing past perfect or real conditionals is not required to get a job but a few basics wouldn't hurt as I was asked about grammar in one interview and asked to demonstrate an on-the-spot lesson in another. One school owner told me that she didn't care about the type of University or major, she only cared about the individual's personality, disposition, common sense, speaking ability and ability to deal with people. **Owners and students want smiling, friendly, competent teachers.**

10

STEP 6

FINDING AN APARTMENT

Finding permanent housing independently is almost impossible. Foreign rooming houses are available but they are essentially expensive dormitories and they are located only in a few places. For the same rent, we are able to enjoy an apartment with our own kitchen and bath near our school but we need help. The school will have a place for us or help us find a place. It will probably be fully furnished. There are also some foreign agencies that will rent to foreigners at a premium. So our school or foreign agencies are our best friend in this respect.

To find an apartment on our own, we need a Japanese guarantor who will guarantee payment of the rent for a 2-year contract. The rent will be at market price and reasonable but the upfront payment will include deposit, agents fee, insurance cost, owners gift money. We will have to pay the equivalent of 4 or 5 months rent as we sign the contract and probably will not get any of it back when we move out. It will not be furnished and we must buy all our own furniture. On the other hand, the apartment will be very clean and refurbished.

Comparatively speaking, if we rent independently, the rent would be lower and the initial payment will be higher than that of the school/agency. After one year, the total payments for renting 1) independently or 2) through a school/agency - would be about the same. However, in the second year renting independently would be cheaper because the monthly rent is lower. The rent is lower because it does not include any commission.

RENTAL EXAMPLE – Initial payment in yen for a comparable apartment.

	SCHOOL/AGENCY	INDEPENDENT
Deposit	30,000	60,000(2)
Agents Fee		30,000(2)
Insurance		15,000(2)
Owners Gift		60,000(2)
Monthly Rent	70,000(1)	55,000
TOTAL	100,000 =($1000)	220,000 =($2200)

1) includes commission of 15,000 (amounts vary)
2) usually not refunded (amounts and policies vary)

If you plan to stay for less than 2 years as most teachers do, then it makes sense to just stay with the school or agency. If you plan to stay longer, can commit to a longer rental contract term and can find a guarantor look into renting independently.

PART IV

11

SQUID AND MAYONNAISE PIZZA

One of the joys in life is eating and in the Tokyo plains where 30 million people reside, there are a large variety of restaurants. The supermarkets also have high quality, reasonably priced food and it compares equally to American products although the portions here are much smaller. Bread loaves, snack bags, and milk cartons and many goods are half the size of American products. Japanese often comment that products in American markets and restaurants are too big.

Three differences from American markets are the bread, cereal and frozen food sections. We can't find the numerous brown breads or large variety of cereal and frozen dinners that are sold stateside. Plain white bread is popular. The seafood section is large, vegetables are cheap but fruits are expensive.

A lot of American food is available at expensive foreign food stores or cheap discount warehouses that have recently come to Japan.

- Pizza toppings may include corn, mayonnaise, squid, potatoes, seaweed, bananas, ice cream, boiled chicken eggs and fish eggs. Potato, mayonnaise and ham pizza is great. Don't count out the boiled egg pizza until you have tried it!
- High fat milk is preferred here. It is hard to find skim milk. Many Japanese people like the taste of high fat milk.
- Beef bowl (fatty beef on rice) shops are popular because they are cheap, fast and delicious. Men and a few ladies sit on counters and 'fast eat' the fast food.
- American or American-like fast food restaurants are at every station. No mash potatoes, but lots of localized hamburger-fried egg combo sandwiches.
- Italian restaurants serve pasta with seaweed, fish eggs, or soy sauce.
- Many restaurants display food with plastic, colored replicas. The actual food served may or may not look like the replicas.
- A lot of cigarette smoke in restaurants and coffee shops. For a smoker, it is convenient, as cigarettes are cheap and easy to buy (many vending machines). There are a few non-smoking sections (but we know how well that works). Well it is better than nothing.

Some men smoke while they walk so the crowded sidewalks are smoky and from time to time an adult body or a child's face gets burned. As a result, some wards in Tokyo have banned smoking in public. Smokers must now smoke in a restaurant or building, or face being fined.

- Half of the restaurant food here is Chinese including fried rice, won ton, pot stickers, ramen, dim sum and meat buns.
- Convenience stores are at every corner and sell tea, lunchboxes, pastry, beer, fishcake, pasta, pickled vegetables, rice balls and buckwheat noodles.
- Root beer is sold only in foreign stores. Most Japanese don't drink it. Some people think it is a type of beer or it tastes like medicine.
- Supermarkets do not have express lines. All the lines are created equal and all customers are treated equally. On special sale days, I have to wait among the housewives and their carts full of groceries to buy one bottle of water. But the carts are only 1/3 the size of US carts.
- Street stands sell the immensely popular ovoid octopus bread balls covered with brown steak-like sauce and dried shaved bonito fish flakes. Six are eaten at one serving with a toothpick.
- Being an onion ring maniac, I am always searching for the perfect ring. It started during my college days when I part-timed at a drive-through near old Honolulu Stadium. I usually eat a few rings absolutely plain and then whack the rest with ketchup gobs. I love

ketchup. I am a ketchup supermaniac. Did you know the etymology of ketchup. It is from the Chinese word 'ke siap'. I am an English teacher. I know these things. Have you eaten ketchup and rice? I did. How about squirting ketchup in a bag of potato chips? It's so good.

Word	Etymology
Ketchup	Chinese (ke tsiap)
Onion	Latin (unio)
Ring	Old English (hring)

Anyway, back to the rings. One day I bought some golden rings but when I bit into it, it was squid rings. Surprise! Now I ask first.

- Tipping is not done here. It is already factored into the price.
- In the teachers' room during lunch, the Aussie teachers like vegemite and the British teachers like brown sauce. Both taste pretty good. Yet these teachers shriek because Americans eat peanut butter and jelly sandwiches. They don't mix the two. Try it, mates! It's fine.
- Near Tokyo train station, I ate at a sandwich shop. I ate standing in the dinning area because there were no chairs. Along the wall there was a bench seat and several tables next to it. On the other side of the tables, no chairs. For some families, one person sat on the bench and the other person STOOD on the other side of the table while they ate. All the tables were taken, half the people sitting on the bench

side, half of them standing on the opposite side of the tables. There were also some stomach-high tables without chairs. Here I ate my fish sandwich, fruit cup and water. The food was very good and I enjoyed my lunch. I could eat while I was standing but I think my legs were confused as usually they get to rest while I eat.

- Japanese often say that American desserts such as cakes, pies and ice cream are too sweet. In fact, American desserts are sweeter than Japanese ones as Japanese desserts are very light and mild. On the other hand, while American entrees are not sweet, Japanese ones such as sukiyaki (beef and vegetables), teriyaki beef (marinated meat), yakitori (barbecue chicken on skewers) and nikujaga (meat and potatoes) are a bit on the sugary side. At the end of the day, the sweetness scale comparing Japanese and American 'soup to nuts' would break even.
- Corn bread is bread with whole kernels of corn.

MY TOP 5 RECOMMENDATIONS

FOOD

1. Shrimp tempura bowl – 'tendon'
2. Japanese curry stew – 'curlei rice'
3. Noodles with pork bone soup – 'tonkotsu ramen'
4. Ginger pork – 'shogayaki'
5. Chestnut cake – 'marron keki'

INTERNATIONAL FOOD IN JAPAN

- Is American fast food international? In Japan, we can eat at American restaurants including burgers, ribs, fried chicken, steak, potato skins, big sandwiches and tacos. In the good old USA, we never take a second look at the local fast food or chain restaurant but here these restaurants are like an oasis in the sea of tranquility? I'm running out of analogies. Anyway, it is good stuff. I'm starting to write like I talk. For hotcakes and sausage, I will get up early on my day-off. For rare prime rib with au jus and lobster tail with butter, I will ride on the packed train for two hours.
- British and Irish Pubs have fish and chips, roasts and meat (pot) pies. Some of these pubs show soccer on big screens.
- Australian Rules football is shown in some bars.
- Canadian restaurants celebrate their Thanksgiving in October.
- Some Asian restaurants serve Thai spicy soup, Vietnamese Pho, and Korean Bi Bim Bop.
- Is Chinese and Italian food considered American food? I think eating take-out Chinese and Pizza is part of American culture. I dream about Chinese Take-out and Pizza To-Go. How about pizza and (American) football. (In Japan and much of the world, football means soccer.) I think the key to this part of American culture is the Chinese take-out or Pizza delivery BOX. The food must be served in a simple mostly white (no lavender please) colored box and after we

are full we can leave the box open on the table until the next morning like we see in the cool televisions sitcoms or movies. In Japan, there are Chinese restaurants galore and Pizza delivery shops abound. Pizza is usually delivered to my apartment in 20 minutes and it's a little pricey but no tip is needed. Sure, the food is important, but I'm happy if it is in a decent box.

RESTAURANT DOS AND DON'TS

DO

Slurp noodles

Try to pay for the bill

Pour alcohol for everyone

Okay to get drunk with associates

Give small gifts to associates

Hold the rice bowl while you eat

Eat curry and rice with a spoon

Say 'Itadakimasu' (I will partake) before eating

Say 'Gochiso sama deshita' (meal was delicious) after eating

DON'T

Put soy sauce on the rice

Drink beer from the bottle

Spear food with the chopsticks

Hover over the group plate with chopsticks while choosing food
Stick the chopsticks upright in a bowl of rice
Pour your own drink from the pitcher to the glass
Pass food from chopstick to chopstick
Lick the chopsticks

INTRIGUING VENDING MACHINES

Live lobster – grab it with the mechanical crane if you can
Hot noodles – is there a cook in there?
Rice balls – at highway car rest stops
Beer – drinking age is 20, 'ID please'
Heated Octopus bread balls – popular snack
Fresh Flowers – in case you need them after midnight
Ladies underwear – who is buying this?
Printclub – self-photos are a craze among schoolgirls.

LIBATION

If you like to drink, this is the country for you.
- Japanese say the drinking together is a type of communication tool especially for business relationships.
- The adjective 'strong' instead of 'heavy' is used to describe the drinker and as the word connotes, it is a good attribute. A man

saying ' I am a strong drinker' is proud and others will be impressed by this admirable trait.
- Office workers often play drinking games at the local bar
- Friday is the big drinking day for workers and students. The bars are crowded and late at night the taxi lines are long.
- Drinking age is 20 but some of them, like us drank when we were teenagers anyway.
- 'Nomi Ho Dai' is a bar special that offers patrons all-you-can-drink for 2 hours.
- Most people catch the train therefore they don't need to worry about driving. If drinkers miss the last train (around midnight), there are several alternatives; a) catch a taxi b) stay in a capsule hotel c) sleep in the station or park d) go to the karaoke box, or e) sit in the bar until morning.

MY TOP 5 RECOMMEDED DRINKS

DRINKS
1. Grape cocktail – 'casshis sour'
2. Cold sake –'sumitai sake'
3. Draft beer – 'nama bee-ehru' (cold and strong)
4. Peach juice – 'momo juice'
5. Cherry-like fruit juice - 'acerola juice'

12

MINI-MINI SKIRTS

High schoolgirls wear mini-mini skirts in summer and freezing winter. After school they roll up their skirts at the waist to make their skirts even shorter as they feel it is fashionable and it make their legs look longer. When they walk up the stairs, they hold their school bags behind them to cover their vulnerable posteriors. In winter they wear heavy short coats, wool scarves and can't-be-shorter skirts. These hardy females also wear long white baggy socks that they glue to their calves to keep them from dropping to their ankles. They use special glue made just for this purpose.

- Some people have brown-dyed hair, blond hair, afros or dreadlocks. Cabin attendants are prohibited from coloring their hair. Hair presentation seems important.
- Appropriately symbolic of a nation's way of thinking, most employees don a uniform. Companies, department stores and train employees all have uniforms. They look quite nice.

- Some young men trim their eyebrows or use make-up.
- Crucifixes and rosaries are worn for fashion only. I was surprised to see some young people wearing full rosaries around their neck.

TRADITIONAL CLOTHES YOU SHOULD SEE OR WEAR

- Yukata (women's colorful summer kimono)
- Girls fluffy kimono on Coming of Age Day (mid January)
- Sumotori (wrestlers) in FULLY-clothed designed traditional wear
- After-bath robes at Onsen Hot Spring (Be careful! Tie the robe tightly or it will open!)

13

DEFINITELY NOT A LAW SCHOOL

But it sure seems like it at the local Westerners' drinking establishment when Westerners from America, Australia, England, Canada, New Zealand and South Africa start spouting their bombastic opinions and debating or joking about every topic imaginable. Even if we are the most liberal Americans we will become more patriotic than we have ever been in our lives as some people like America and some do not. Consequently, we, in an involuntary, almost Pavlovian, All-American response, will find ourselves unequivocally defending our home and fellow Americans.

Some people from other countries say they don't care for the American system but they like American people and culture. Nowadays, Americans seem to be receiving more criticism than giving it so don't be surprised if you have to play defense when you find yourself out on the conversational gridiron. Despite this, Westerners have many things in common and we are like a family away from home. Moreover, our diversity makes us stronger.

As US citizens we will find ourselves saying the word 'American' many times whereas back home our nationality is a given and unless we are watching the Olympics, we identify ourselves more by city and state. In this worldly setting, we gradually learn a bit about international diplomacy.

In tandem with the battle of polar views is the invaluable process of learning about other countries, states, people and culture from its real live (albeit transplanted) citizens. The opportunity to share in this forum is rare and the learning curve is steep. Beliefs, conceptions and stereotypes will be dashed or confirmed and as a result we can not only learn about Japan but other countries as well.

In summary, Westerners really enjoy talking and joking with each other in the neighborhood pub. After all, it is an oasis of English and our thirst to hear and speak our native language in a foreign land often needs to be quenched.

NATIONALITIES OF WESTERNERS SAMPLED

American	26%
Australian	26
Canadian	21
British	13
New Zealander	9
Scottish	5

Total   <u>100%</u>

Notes:

1) The above represents a random sampling of English-speakers some of who are teachers working in Japan. I have also known a teacher from South Africa.

2) There are many types and sizes of English schools. There are some schools that just have American teachers that teach American English or British teachers that teach British English. Some schools recruit teachers that speak only North American (American and Canadian) English. Smaller schools may have one or two teachers and it is up to the owners' discretion who to hire. Large schools tend to be cosmopolitan. .

3) Fellow Americans are friendly and fun. Some of the British teachers that I have met are very polite and well mannered. Some Canadians that I have met are cool. Some of the Australians and New Zealanders that I have met are very charismatic and attractive. When we get together, we seem to adopt each other's English. Some Australians begin to use an American accent. Some Americans start using Australian English such as 'How was your holiday (vacation)?' or 'No worries' or 'Pass me the vegemite' (it tastes good). By the way, thanks mates for teaching me Australian ('Oss-tr-eye-lian'). But I still have a hard time understanding the 'Down Under' magazines because of the accent. Maybe I should read silently.

14

THE HAND THAT GROPES AND OTHER SEXUAL SUBJECTS

Explicit magazine photos of young nubile girls are on display in the convenience stores. Bosomy bikini-clad models spot the walls on trains and topless girls can easily be seen on the covers of "men's" newspapers, which are quite openly read. But no one usually looks and no one really cares as everyone on the train is either sleeping or emailing frantically on their cell phones.

The morning rush hour trains are impossibly packed. People are squashed and pressed against every conceivable side of the human body. On the train, one can't move and one doesn't need to hold on to anything to keep one's balance as everybody keeps everybody else upright. Our bodies are like public property.

Just when we think there is absolutely no more room, more people press their bodies into the metal container of crammed human flesh. And then yet another dogged businessman will approach the train door already overflowing with bodies. He will face the entrance with his backside. Then with two hands he'll grab the frame above the door and push with his legs to force his body in. Finally the conductor will run over and stuffs him in so the door can close. As the train pulls away, those still on the platform can see the results of this gallant commuter's success; his face pressing against the door glass in an impotently triumphant expression of resignation.

Train passengers on a crowded train usually face the train door therefore late arriving people back in so they won't be face to face with everyone. Once a female was the last one to back in the packed train. The conductor came over to push her in but didn't know what part of her body to push. He couldn't push her breasts or stomach. Nor her thighs. How about her face? Then he simply asked her to turn around so her back would be facing the door and he correctly push her with his hands on her back with all his platform-leveraged might, into the jumbo can of bodies. No foul, No problem.

Just when the train is too full, sweaty and nobody can stand it anymore – out comes a hand. Stories of women being groped on the ridiculously jammed trains are sometimes on television and in the newspaper. I have also heard stories directly from some female victims themselves (who in fact are not hard to find in the metropolis). A Japanese woman told me that, generally speaking, the groper (chikan) positions himself behind the intended victim where he attempts to furtively fondle her. The poor girl, not being able to move in a rush hour train, can't escape. Some women scream, stomp on their foot or many say nothing. The lady in question told me that since she cut her long hair, it hasn't happened again.

Another female commuter stated that a man sat next to her and opened a magazine to hide his actions as he tried to paw her. One female mentioned to me that she was molested on a weekly basis on the morning train when she was in high school and that young women are too afraid to say anything so they don't.

Americans feel danger in isolated places and would, in all likelihood feel safer in a group of suited business people. Here, however danger may lurk in the crowd. On the rush hour train containing among others, many neatly attired working people and students, there is always the possibility of the predatory hand. Furthermore, a fourth woman told me that the morning rush hour is silent and for a young girl to shout out loud takes a lot of courage. She said her friend did a very brave thing when they were in high school, she grabbed the molester's hand and took him to the police station.

In incidences involving Westerners, one female said a man touched her top then ran out of the train. A second one mentioned that she was flashed.

Recently, more and more train companies have started incorporating women-only train cars into their lines. Some train companies have one women-only car at the end of the train.

The fetish impulses of some males are by no means restricted to groping. Stealing underwear from clotheslines has been a topic on television. A lady told me that she called the police when she saw a man taking underwear from her neighbor's clothesline. The perpetrator had a bag full of lingerie.

There have also been news reports of men putting mirrors on their briefcase or video recorders in a handbag to look or film up girl's skirts. 'Enjo kousai' is the term that refers to the arrangement where a man pays a high school girl for a 'date' in a hotel. After midnight, television programs often include sensual animation, miniskirts comedies and bikinis games.

15

TEACHER-STUDENT PROFILES, SURVEY AND TYPES

AVERAGE TEACHER PROFILE

Name: Mike
Nationality: American
Race: German
Age: 29
Sex: Male
Status: Single
University major: Bachelor of Art-Literature
Previous Job: Salesman for a frozen food company
Reason for coming to Japan: Work and travel
Interests: computers, reading, hiking

Name: Lauren
Nationality: Australian
Race: English-Italian-Irish
Age: 24
Sex: Female
Status: Single
University major: Bachelor of Science-Psychology
Previous Job: None – just graduated from Uni (university)
Reason for coming to Japan: Save money and travel
Interests: music and movies

AVERAGE STUDENT PROFILE
Name: Yuko
Nationality: Japanese
Race: Japanese
Age: 25
Sex: Female
Status: Single
University major: Bachelor of Law
Job: Office lady for Import Company
Reason for studying English: Talk to foreigners
Interests: shopping and music
English fluency: Beginner

Name: Takeshi

Nationality: Japanese

Race: Japanese

Age: 38

Sex: Male

Status: Married with 1 daughter

University major: Bachelor of Computer Science

Job: System Engineer for Computer Company

Reason for studying English: Work

Interests: Baseball

English fluency: Intermediate

Note: These profiles above represent composites of some teachers in the greater Tokyo area and students that I have taught privately. They don't represent any specific individuals.

SURVEY

<u>WESTERNER</u>   <u>JAPANESE</u>

1. Favorite Japanese Food
    1. Sushi   1. Sushi
    2. Tempura   2. Natto-fermented beans

    3. Pork Cutlet   3. Tempura
2. Favorite Non-Japanese Food
    1. Italian   1. Spaghetti
    2. American   2. Chinese
    3. Steak   3. Hamburger
3. Strangest Food Eaten
    1. Monkey brain   1. Crocodile
    2. Chocolate ants   2. Snake soup
    3. Frog   3. Raw Squid intestines
4. Food that made you sick
    1. Locusts   1. Crab
    2. Oysters   2. Oysters
    3. Fish   3. Curry
5. What language you want to speak other than English
    1. Japanese   1. French
    2. Spanish   2. Chinese
    3. Chinese   3. Italian
6. Most Desirable qualities in a Man
    1. Humor   1. Kindness
    2. Kindness   2. Good Character
    3. Smile   3. Bravery
7. Most Desirable qualities in a Woman
    1. Looks   1. Kindness
    2. Humor   2 Affection

3. Kindness 3. Intelligence

8. What is your dream job?
    1. Writer   1. Translator
    2. Actor   2. Cabin Attendant
    3. Scuba Instructor 3. Tour Guide

9. Favorite place to visit in Japan
    1. Kyoto   1. Hokkaido
    2. Sapporo   2. Kyoto
    3. Kamakura   3. Nagasaki

10. Favorite place to visit other than Japan
    1. California   1. America
    2. Thailand   2 England
    3. Hong Kong   3. Canada

11. Happiest age in life
    1. 21   1. 23
    2. 28   2. 25
    3. 24   3. 19

12. What you do when you feel stress or sad
    1. Eat Junk Food   1. Talk
    2. Drink   2. Exercise
    3. Exercise   3. Drink

14. What you do on the train
    1. Read   1. Read
    2. Email   2 Sleep

114

3. Watch People	3. Email

15. Something you like about Japan

1. People	1. Safety
2. Safety	2. People
3. Culture	3. Food

16. What time you take a shower

1. 10:00 a.m.	1. 8:00 p.m.
2. 11:30 a.m.	2. 10:00 p.m.
3. 5:00 p.m.	3. 11:00 p.m.

Note: The survey above was taken from Westerners and Japanese in Japan.

TEACHER TYPES (found at the local watering hole)

1. Dialog Man seeks conversational domination of the bar with his anecdotes and long monologues but on the other hand, the atmosphere might not be so interesting without him.
2. Cultural Sensei enjoys wearing a yukata (summer kimono), visiting temples and playing the shakuhachi (flute).
3. Real Teacher majored in education and has teaching experience.
4. What's-Your-Email-Address teacher likes to socialize with teachers, students and citizens.
5. Traveling Instructor is away traveling or making plans to travel.

STUDENT TYPES (private students I have taught)
1. You-Can-Hear-Rice-Growing student is quiet. The teacher learns to befriend silence.
2. Human Dictionary loves English and knows some vocabulary and grammar rules that the teacher doesn't know. He may say 'Pluralization definitely may be imminent.'
3. Wealthy Housewife has been married many years and enjoys her free time. She may give generous gifts to the teacher.
4. Friendly International Single Girl has traveled to many countries. Her consumption is important to the GDP (Gross Domestic Product) of several countries. She is very friendly to the teacher.
5. Dedicated Salaryman is cordial but serious about improving his English. He works 12-14 hours a day.
6. Pleasure-to-Teach student may not be fluent in English but because he tries so hard, the teacher admires his effort.

Homestay Girl was a quiet, shy Masters student. She traveled to North America for a one-year stay. When she returned to Japan, she had drastically transformed. To my uncomfortable surprise, she had become plump and although she was still a nice person, she was loud and used many slang words.

'Let's party dude' she blurted as she gestured and tilted her body. Several months later, she had become slim and quiet again.

16

THE RESTROOM KNOCK

In the metropolis, a small percentage of the toilets are western. Some of the department stores have high-tech heated seats and bidets. Watery soap or soapy foam is occasionally available to cleanse our hands. Paper towels are rare, blow dryers are common and certain restrooms have nothing. We just have to let the water evaporate. Often there is a common entrance for everyone then the walkway splits for men and ladies. Don't be surprised if an elderly cleaning lady is standing next to you tidying up the restroom.

In Japan, the toilet stall's wall and door extend all the way to the floor. In America, Japanese are surprised when they go to toilets which have a gap between the wall and the floor and its gives us the option to peek at our neighbors dropped wrinkled pants. In America, when we want to use the toilet we can see that the door is closed or we are able to see under the stall. But in Japan, since the wall extends all the way to the floor we can't see if anyone is there. Therefore when a Japanese citizen wants to enter a stall and find out if it is vacant, he will knock on the closed door to check if someone is in there. Don't be offended, he doesn't want to join you. If you are in the stall, just knock once or twice on the door in response and the person will leave you alone. The first time someone knocked on the door of my stall I didn't know what was going on so I just said 'Yo!'

I'm not going to get into the mechanics of using a Japanese toilet because I don't really want to think or write about it but the following is required to use it.

- Courage (especially at FIRST sight)
- Strong legs and bendable knees
- Balance
- Indigestion or no time to find a western one

If you dare to try the Japanese no-seat style toilet, hold on to the wall and be sure you don't fall in. Take care.

17

MOVIES BY ANOTHER TITLE

The tickets prices here are two or three times the price of American movie tickets while popcorn and soda prices are about the same as the US. As a result, my popcorn, hot dog and soda snack actually cost less than the movie ticket. Most of the movies seen in Japan are shown three to six months after they debut in America and are subtitled with Japanese. Because the English title is often difficult for Japanese to understand, there is also a Japanese movie title to make the movie theme more understandable. I think these titles in Japan are interesting especially the ones the are completely different.

American Title	Japanese Title(translated)
Movies	
Analyze This	Analyze Me
Planet of the Apes	Monkey's Planet
Enemy of the State	Enemy of America

Death Wish II	Los Angeles
Enter the Dragon	Fighting Dragon
Married to the Mob	Beloved Mafia
In the Line of Fire	The Secret Service
When We were Kings	Muhammad Ali's Precious Days
Witness	Detective John Book's Witness
Sudden Impact	Dirty Harry 4
The Devil's Own	Devil
Forest Gump	Once in a Lifetime Chance
Miss Congeniality	Dangerous Beauty
The Princess Diaries	Pretty Princess
War of the Worlds	Space War

Television

The West Wing	The White House
Aly Mcbeal	Aly My love
Bewitched	My Wife is a Witch

18

WHICH IS MORE PRIMITIVE CHICKEN OR FISH?

In Japanese supermarket I have never seen a chicken drumstick and rarely a leg or a whole chicken. There are wings and drumlets but almost all chicken is sold boneless because bones and skins are considered too animal-like and unappetizing. One man told me that he couldn't eat chicken if it had skin or bone or looked like chicken. He could only eat it if it was in fried, breaded and shaped like a nugget and didn't look anything like chicken.

No beef bones either. I have never seen a T-bone steak, rib steak, prime rib roast or rack of ribs. Just meat with the bones butchered off. Only meat that is perfectly cut, clean, and of high enough quality is put on display.

On the other hand, fish and most organisms that live in the sea whether raw, cooked, whole, filleted, just killed or still moving are all eaten. The fresher the better and the more recently alive the more delectable, (or so it's said). It's a seafood eating country and it is one of the reasons why the diet is low in fat and lives are long.

Stateside, we like our birds with skin, bone or whole and our fish very still and very cooked. I like to eat half a barbecue chicken with my dirty hands. Sounds fishy? Well okay enough fowl language. Whoops! Hahaha…Brahahaha…

RECOMMENDATIONS FOR FISH AND CHICKEN
- Raw tuna sushi with green horseradish - 'maguro with wasabe'
- Grilled saury fish - 'samma shioyaki'
- Deep fried boneless chicken pieces - 'karagay''
- Teriyaki minced chicken balls on skewers - 'tsukune'
- Skewered chicken with salt - 'yakitori'

Note: The Japanese make an exception at Christmas time. Their typical modern Christmas dinner is a baked, fried or teriyaki chicken leg. It is sold in the market or restaurants especially and only for Christmas. Since turkey is not popular in Japan, the chicken leg dinner is their version of the American turkey dinner.

9

CAPSULE HOTEL

The local koban (police station) officer drew me a map of the hotel's location which was about 2 minutes from the station. It was about 11:00 p.m. and the street barkers were out fishing for customers.

The entrance of the hotel was bright and clean. In order to approach the carpeted front desk lobby, I had to slide off my shoes. From the capsule layout map, I chose capsule number 122. I recommend choosing one that is far from the main door and one on the 2nd tier. It is quieter, higher and it feels more secure. I locked my shoes in shoe locker (122), located in the lobby and gave the shoe locker key to the front desk clerk and paid 3800 yen ($35). The clerk gave me another key, the clothes locker key (122) that was attached to a plastic wristband. In the locker room, I locked all my clothes and belongings in a narrow metal locker and slipped into the hotel's prison-orange pajamas and then looked for the bath. I walked through a semi-lit corridor to the bathroom with only a towel and key faithfully dangling from my wrist.

The group bath had everything. In the body-scrubbing section, I sat on a one-foot plastic stool and washed and shampooed using liquid soap and a small spray hose conveniently placed for the earnest bather like myself.

A question flashed through my soap-addled brain. Why is it, I wondered, that Japanese sit down to shower yet stand up to eat noodles while Americans stand up to shower but sit down to eat noodles? And why do Japanese spend a long time taking a shower and bath but eat very quickly while Americans take fast showers but take a long time to eat? Different priorities, I guess.

Disposable razors were in a small container and I shaved facing the mirror with the other bathers. The other patrons were minding their own bubbly business and no one made lengthy eye contact so I didn't feel uncomfortable. As customary, after taking the seated shower, some very clean bodies entered the steaming bath pool and soaked until done.

The capsule holding room was dim and plausibly serene. Along the wall, there were two tiers of capsules. My number was 122 so I had to climb up into a body-size tunnel with only a curtain covering the one entrance. In the capsule, there was a pancaked pillow, green blanket, paper-book sized TV, a broken radio, tissues and small trash box. A pay TV featuring adult programs was sitting forlornly in the corner. The comfort level was pretty good. The temperature was cool and the mattress was soft. It wasn't so claustrophobic and I slept comfortably.

Since checkout time was 10:00am, I shaved, brushed my teeth and got dressed. At the front desk, I returned my clothes locker key and they gave me my shoe locker key. With my shoes now liberated, I was ready to leave. At 10:05, I felt refreshed and reentered the mass of people on the bustling street. While it may be true that I haven't climbed Mount Fuji, made a pilgrimage around Shikoku or seen the ice castles of Sapporo, at least I have slept in a capsule hotel.

20

THE CASE OF THE MISSING WESTERNERS

On the average, many Westerners in Japan stay for about a year. Some of them leave within a month, not liking the lifestyle. Others stay longer, especially those who have careers, are married to Japanese citizens or enjoy the lifestyle. However, once in a while, on any given day, without notice or explanation, someone from the English-speaking community suddenly disappears.

- Over the years, more than one Westerner has gone on vacation to their home country and has never come back.
- A female vacationed in Europe, returned to Japan and after a few days suddenly left Japan never to return.

- After two months of work, a newly arrived man disappeared from his job and his home, leaving his wife and his two young daughters behind.

The English-speaking community is small and connected. Today's breaking news got here yesterday. The grapevine is fast. With news like this, it is 'speculation city.' Several months later, we may hear from a source of a source about the real story. If it is amazing and plausible, we want to believe it.   But is it the real story? Sometimes the case is just never 'solved.'

WESTERNERS' NUMBER OF YEARS WORKED IN JAPAN

4 or more years	22%
3 years	9
2	26
1	13
Less than 1 year	30
Total	100%

Note: The above table represents a random sampling of Westerners from the English-speaking community at a random point in time. It indicates the years worked in Japan and the percentage of people in each category. The table below represents the same sample.

BREAKDOWN OF YEARS WORKED BY GENDER

	FEMALE	MALE	TOTAL
4 or more years	20%	80%	100%
3	0	100	100
2	33	67	100
1	33	67	100
Less than 1 year	86	14	100

Notes:

1) Based on the above percentages, it appears that males tend to stay longer than female do. Males have commented that possible reasons for this is that more males have careers, are married to Japanese females, have Japanese girlfriends or find it more enjoyable to live here. Some females have said that they have other goals such as travel or work that lead them elsewhere. A blond female stated that she left specifically because of the unwelcome attention she got in public places. Other women have mentioned that it is hard to find a good boyfriend.

2) Every month in Japan, Westerners come and go. This makes the environment very dynamic. Sometimes, a young Westerner leaves and cries and gives a speech, along the lines of, 'I love all you guys, it has been the best experience of my life, I will cherish our

memories forever...' Since it happens so often the veterans think, 'OK whatever, bye.' Well, we're not so cold. We have become better people having known you. Etc. See ya!

21

JAPANESE ENGLISH

Many English words have been assimilated into the Japanese language. The pronunciation and meaning may be quite different, as you can see from the following examples.

JAPANESE	ENGLISH
Skinship	physical friendship
Supa	spa
Suupa	supermarket
Sekuhara	sexual harassment
Dustbox	wastepaper basket
Doriba	screwdriver
Wrecka	wrecker (tow truck)
Mota	motor
Chancesu	chance
Hamburg	hamburger

Stalka	stalker
Cohee	coffee
Curlei lice	curry stew with rice
Terebi	television
Lobu lobu	in love
Igrisu	England
Yorropa	Europe
Furunto garasu	windshield
Raito	lights
Reba	liver
Genghis kahn	barbecue lamb
Hello work	employment agency
Girlhunt	meet girls
Bokushingu	boxing
Taoru	towel
Pantsu	underwear
Reggie	cash register
Chubu	inner tube
Viking	buffet
Katsu	cutlet ('cutletsu')
Biya gaden	beer garden (bar)
Virgin road	aisle (church wedding)

ANNOUNCEMENT

'Thanks you for you coming'

FASCINATING SIGNS

'No smoking sheet' – No smoking seat

'Clap Shop' – Crepe Shop

'Pain Shop' – Pan (bread) Shop

'Clean Energie' – Landry shop

'Club You' - Bar

TRANSLATIONS

COMMON ENGLISH	COMMON JAPANESE	LITERAL TRANSLATION
Statue of Liberty	'Jiyu no megami'	Freedom's goddess
Bullet train	'Shinkansen'	New trunk line

FAMOUS DISTRICT

Ginza means 'Official silver site'

FOREIGNER

The correct word for foreigner is 'gaikokugin'. The word often used is 'gaigin' but it is considered inappropriate and impolite.

ORANGE JUICE

Early in the 20th Century, many Japanese emigrated to other countries, including Brazil. A Cabin attendant said that some Brazilians of Japanese ancestry speak the traditional Japanese that was used when their ancestors left Japan many years ago. For example, when ordering orange juice they say 'mikan sui' (meaning 'orange water') using Japanese words used many years ago. But now in Japan, some words have become westernized so Japanese always say 'orange juice.'

22

IMAGE OF AMERICA

While living here I have met many Japanese people including university students, teachers, businessmen, company presidents, housewives, office ladies, truck drivers, cooks, the unemployed, hostesses, cabin attendants and foreign nationals. They seem to say similar things about America.

- America is dangerous.
- America is big.
- Americans have guns.
- American people are big and food portions are too big, too greasy, and too sweet.
- American food is hot dogs and hamburgers.
- Americans are white or black.

A young Japanese man told me that he wasn't comfortable in New York City because there were too many 'non-American-looking' people. He said he preferred Chicago because they had 'real' Americans.

When I was looking for an apartment, I went with a Scandinavian rental manager to visit his Asian-Canadian tenant. A Japanese repairman was there and, just by sight, he thought the manager was American and the tenant was from China. It is not uncommon for people to have these misconceptions about other countries and their people. In a homogeneous country, however, it is likely that misconceptions breed and linger. To this repairman, it's a simple world, all Caucasians are American and all non-Japanese Asians are Chinese.

Some Japanese people think that America is dangerous and that everyone has a gun. This image is so powerful that some Japanese will not visit America. They would rather go to a 'safer' country. Among English-speaking countries, some Japanese travelers choose 'safe' countries like Australia or Canada.

I have responded to these concerns by saying that many Americans know the dangerous places and the dangerous times and avoid them. For example, dark isolated places after midnight may be dangerous. In addition, we watch out for dangerous people and try to avoid them. Dangerous people can cause problems whether they have a gun or not (when some people think about America, they think - Guns.) We can't deny that there is some danger. However, it is a small part that is overshadowed by many of the other great things about America.

Some people's image of America comes from movies, television and the news media. The influence of movies is very strong. In addition, the news here is the same as it is anywhere - sensational. Much of the news about America is about crime. Additionally, moviegoers sometimes believe that movies are real. Once a man believed something was a historical fact because he saw it in a movie.

It is natural to respond to certain cues based on the images we have developed throughout our lives, especially if they were formed when we were young and impressionable. Certain images are like night dreams - people think they are real or want them to be real.

QUESTIONS I HAVE BEEN ASKED AS AN AMERICAN

- Do you drink raw eggs like in the movie Rocky?
- Do you have a gun?
- Have you ever been held up?
- Can you use chopsticks?
- Do you eat a hamburger everyday?
- Do pineapples grow on trees?

Note:

1) I have drunk raw eggs in a health shake many moons ago, but would never do it now. In Japan, I have eaten as Japanese do (sukiyaki meat dipped in scrambled raw eggs). It is fantastic.

2) Yes, pineapples grow on trees. I'm joking. Let me flip-flop (a term used in American Elections). No, they don't. They grow on a crown of thin, narrow leaves close to the ground. Another crown grows on top of the pineapple. This new crown can be planted in the ground and another pineapple will grow. How do I know? I planted a crown in our backyard when I was a kid, and grew a homegrown pineapple. In addition, I worked at the pineapple cannery for two high school summers. I worked with whole pineapples, slices, juice, tibbits and chunks. Pineapple-Canadian Bacon (non-Hawaiians call this Hawaiian pizza) pizza is the best.

23

HAWAIIAN EATS

Some thoughts of living in Japan.

There is some Hawaiian food here:

1) Loco moco – sunny-side up egg and hamburger patty on two scoops of steamed white rice and macaroni salad covered with brown gravy. Here teriyaki sauce is used.
2) There are expensive macadamia nuts and passion fruit juice in the department stores
3) Mahi-mahi sandwiches and guava juice are served at some restaurants

Canned luncheon meat is popular in Hawaii and it can be bought in the foreign food section of Japanese supermarkets or Okinawan stores. I am not a canned luncheon meat historian but I believe it became popular in Hawaii and Okinawa after World War II because it was not only tasty but also inexpensive and easy to buy. Nowadays, Okinawans eat this meat stir-fried with bitter melon.

Being a typical Hawaiian, I am a canned luncheon meat lover and like it plain right out of the can.

Note: My favorite traditional Hawaiian food is Laulau, which I can't find here. It is pork and fish wrapped in taro leaves. Compliment it with some poi (cold mashed taro) and guava juice and I'll be content. That did it, now I'm hungry!

PART V

24

THE FUTURE

One can only speculate about the future.

- Consumption tax of 5% will probably increase
- The working population will decrease and the aging population will increase
- English teaching will continue to thrive
- Westernization of culture and young people continues
- To supplement the working population, restrictions on foreign immigration may be eased
- Other Asian nations economies will be increasingly competitive
- Prices will decrease because of deflation, competition and movement toward a market economy.

Note: Many Japanese that I have talked to were not so optimistic about the future as they are worried about the decreasing working population, pension problems, taxes and economic competition in Asia. The future is hard to predict yet the current standard of living seems good.

25

REASONS TO STAY A WHILE

WE CAN GO.

The first reason to stay is that we can go. We can leave anytime at the end of our contract or even before with a month's notice. Freedom allows us to move to another city, country or back home. Having this liberty takes some burden off our minds and, for the noncommittal free spirit, it is quite comforting. Some teachers return to their home country, miss living in Japan and come back again. Others have been 'leaving' Japan for years, only to postpone the return home a little longer. There are many reasons to stay.

A NEW LIFE

The multi-act drama of living unfolds quickly around here with so many developments taking place every day. Suddenly a new life and new world with good friends, coworkers, a job, money, a homey apartment and purchased stuff is born. In no time, one feels a sense of belonging. In some cases, serious relationships or careers develop and there is much more reason to stay and enjoy this Eastern chapter in our lives.

THE JOB

Many hours are spent at our jobs and, as a consequence, we can be satisfied if we are able to find the following:

    1) Enough money- salaries are adequate here and, for those who don't go out every night, saving isn't a problem. For Americans, money shouldn't be the primary reason to come here. The salary is modest and the exchange rate is not favorable, but the tax rate is low. The average salary is $30,000 a year and you can make more if you also have private students or business classes. Overall the salaries are pretty good.

    2) Job Satisfaction – This can be found in a number of ways.

        Feeling challenged – always something new

Provide a useful service – help people with a new skill

Like our work – enjoyable

Are appreciated – students thank us and sometimes we receive gifts. Teachers have said they have occasionally received expensive gifts such as $100 gift certificates, or tie pins or brand name bags and we often receive small gifts, such as chocolates or cookies. I have found that private students are like friends so they are inclined to give generous gifts. I have received gift certificates, books, dishes and baked lobster tail!

3) Pleasant working environment – In the universe of all possible jobs, some have long hours with low stress while others have normal hours with high stress. Others are hourly. Teaching has normal hours (about 35 a week) with an average amount of stress. It is more similar to an hourly job than a project-oriented one, and teachers are paid commensurately. When we leave for the night, duties do not carry over to the next day. Many schools are fairly new, carpeted, temperature controlled for the hot summers and cold winters. Most teachers leave school within 10

minutes after the last class is finished. Generally, there are no deadlines or projects to complete.

4) Good Teaching Management – Frankly, I am surprised at how progressive the teaching management is for some schools. It is not the top-down management style that I envisioned would be practiced in Japan's vertical society. Teachers are given a generous amount of freedom, and their input is welcomed. Westerners manage Westerners and in many cases, bosses are more like friends in a community where there are relatively few of us and we are all far from home. If the management is Japanese, teachers may have to conform to a more traditional, autocratic style. Leaders know that a happy teacher is more likely to be a good teacher, and in an industry where the teacher's performance is tantamount to a schools success, schools try to help teachers. Having worked at companies in Hawaii and California, including an international accounting firm, insurance companies and a computer company, I have some perspective of work conditions and quality of management and I believe that the management and work conditions here are very good. Of course, we are comparing apples and mandarin oranges as the

industry, type of work and salary are different. Regardless, I feel fortunate to be working with such teaching management.

MONTHLY BUDGET – AN ESTIMATE IN YEN

Minimum monthly Salary	250,000 yen
Tax (5%) varies	12,500
Employment/Health Insurance (3.5%)	8,750
Salary after tax and insurance	228,750

Monthly Expenses
Rent	65,000
Utilities	10,000
Cell Phone	5,000
Food	70,000
Clothes	10,000
Entertainment	20,000
Miscellaneous	10,000
Net Salary after tax, insurance and expenses	38,750

1) Exchange rate.
    If $1.00=100 yen then 38,750 yen = $387.50

If $1.00=110 yen then 38,750 yen = $352.27

2) Japan is experiencing deflation, so salary and prices are not rising. Some prices are falling. Haircuts and household goods have become cheaper. I have asked my landlord to reduce my rent, and it has been reduced twice. Soon, Japan's population will begin decreasing, and this may affect real estate prices and rents.

3) Keep in mind that we are not automatically paying into the Social Security System as we would back home, so we may need to save some money ourselves. For those who stay for only 1 or 2 years, the effect of nonparticipation is immaterial. This is not advice. Please see a retirement professional.

4) As Americans, we are required to file income tax returns on worldwide income, no matter what country we are in. At this time, the minimum forms to file are the 1040 and 2555EZ. English teachers are not highly paid, therefore our income is well below the foreign income exclusion ceiling. If we have lived here for over one year and earn below the exclusion ceiling, it is possible that we may be exempt from US Federal income tax. We are taxed by Japan and the US government may not tax us again unless we earn over the exclusion ceiling. This is not tax advice. See the IRS and your State income tax instructions or talk to your tax professional for more information.

Salary is not high, yet income tax is relatively low, and consequently we can support ourselves and still have some money to save or spend. The average annual salary is about USD$30,000.

TRAVELING

Many teachers have wanderlust and seem to be travelling every other month to other parts of Asia, around the world, back home and around Japan. Other Asian nations are near Nippon and teachers find it enjoyable to vacation there.

Thailand, Korea and Hong Kong are very popular because they are nearby, prices are cheap and the food is exotic and scrumptious. Thailand has spicy soup, Korea has Kal Bi barbecue short ribs and Hong Kong has dim sum. Try Hong Kong's shrimp dumplings ('har gau'). Everyone raves about the cheap and healing Thai massages. I won't forget the brilliant night view of the Hong Kong Island's skyline from Kowloon.

In Japan, almost everyone visits Kyoto for its beautiful temples. Japanese people travel to this city many times. The famous Kinkakuju (golden temple) is stunning and surrounded by a peaceful garden. Because Kyoto has many historic structures, Americans chose not to bomb it during WWII and consequently many temples are still intact. Kyoto was the capital of Japan for many centuries. Later, the capital was moved east to Tokyo. 'To' means 'eastern' and 'kyo' stands for Kyoto meaning 'capital'. Therefore, Tokyo stands for 'Eastern Kyoto' or 'Eastern Capital'.

Teachers often go home for a visit because it is such a treat to visit family, friends and to eat Mom's home-cooked food. When I travel back home to Honolulu, the plane leaves a late Japanese night and gradually flies into an early Hawaiian morning. From darkness, we fly into a mirage of orange, pink and purple colors. This phantasm soon morphs into an elevated ocean of glorious blue air. Below the clouds, green mountains, coastline and legendary surf eventually appear. Finally, the lochs of Pearl Harbor and the battleship brothers, Arizona and Missouri can be seen just before the jet lands at sunny Honolulu airport. It is such a great feeling. I think everyone must feel the same when visiting their own hometown. We seem to appreciate home so much more when we live away.

Airfares are reasonable and airports and airlines are numerous and convenient for the travel addict. Japanese airlines provide excellent service and cabin attendants are friendly to foreigners. Moreover, Immigration and Customs are very fast and efficient. Once when returning to Japan at Narita airport, I de-planed and went to the restroom.. Then I stood in line at immigration for a few minutes and in the customs area I then went to get my suitcase. I couldn't find my suitcase right away because it was already taken off the rotating belt and efficiently given to the nearby airline counter service desk. After retrieving my suitcase, it took only a minute to clear Customs.

MOUNT FUJI

Mount Fuji condescends to the clouds and it is a much wider and more imposing vision than one might imagine. Many teachers climb it every year during the safe summer season. Even then, it is near freezing at the summit. Other seasons are too cold and dangerous. Hikers can ride a bus to the 5th Station and climb for several hours starting at night to see the sunrise. We can also enjoy views of this towering symbol of Japan from the many tourist towns in the vast flatlands encircling it. Many hot springs allow the bather to view this grand volcano while they bathe. It is not extinct and may erupt again someday. If it does, much of greater Tokyo will be covered with lava or ash.

HOT SPRING BATHS (ONSEN)

The water is hot enough to make homo sapien soup, but I prefer remaining raw. To accomplish this luke-warm goal, I enter the private family bath for couples or families at a Japanese Inn. We can lock the door behind us and no one else will enter. These baths are small and intimate, and I can turn on the cold water to bring the temperature down a bit to keep my meat from turning medium rare. Furthermore, I don't really cherish sitting in a large public bath constantly averting my eyes from 20 other naked men.

In this exclusive bath setting, we can do some snorkeling (but we shouldn't), relax and chat at our own leisure. But don't cook too long. It is wise to get out of the simmering pot before too many shrivels show up where they don't belong.

The liquid heat causes us to perspire and after we withdraw from the bath, our bodies feel refreshed and cool. We become hungry enough to eat a whale and in this country, we can. So, it is fitting that the hot spring inn prepare a traditional eye-pleasing, multi-mini dish spread with crab, fish and scallops and icy cold drinks.

Note: In the home, Japanese wash their bodies in a separate shower space and after they are clean, they sit in the adjacent bathtub and soak for a while. All family members do this and soak in the same bath water at different times during the night. The bathtub water is kept warm by an automatic tub heater. The next day the bathtub water is siphoned into the clothes washing machine to wash clothes. Water is used to clean several times.

HISTORY

To understand the present, we must understand the past, and Japan has a long history. Three historical sites worth mentioning lured me with their inviting stories, Nagasaki on Kyushu island, and Ito and Shimoda near Tokyo.

Nagasaki may be the San Francisco of Japan with its undulating hills surrounding a sleepy bay. It has colorful streetcars, an enchanting Chinatown and the site of the second Atomic bomb. The bomb's epicenter is on a modest hillside miles away from its intended target - a bayside shipyard. A huge, green and bulbous replica of the bomb stands ominously in a nearby museum. It exploded high above the ground to cover its designated target. As I walked through the epicenter's flat, grassy field toward a dark, rectangular monument, a school of miniscule, flying insects hovered near my head. I felt uneasy as I imagined the holocaust that occurred at my very feet many years ago. Now, it is a simple park.

Ito is a passive, coastal village that waits three hours from Tokyo on the Izu peninsula. In the 1600s, British citizen William Adams survived the shipwreck of a Dutch ship and subsequently helped the ruling Shogun build a large, seaworthy ship. On the shore where a trickling rivulet assimilates into the sea, there is an abstract, iron statue, walkway mosaic and mini ship model to mark the accomplishment. As we posed for pictures near the statue, I could imagine the wooden ship being built on the shore with the beautiful Izu coastline dominating the background.

Further south on the same peninsula of Izu naps the scenic Baytown of Shimoda where Commodore Matthew Calbraith Perry, steamed his lethal, muscle-bound flotilla of 'black ships' in February 1854 to persuade the xenophobic Shogunate to open Japan. Nippon had been closed to the world for hundreds of years as Japan's lords felt that outside influence especially the teachings of Christianity, would upset the rigid, hierarchical structure of its society. American President Filmore, however, believed it was an appropriate time to initiate diplomatic relations.

In a letter President Filmore made several requests:

1) Begin international trading
2) shipwrecked sailors be treated well
3) establish friendship between the two nations
4) ships be able to stop for coal and provisions

The Kanagawa Treaty, then was signed ending Nippon's autarky. As I strolled along the bay, I could see in my mind's eye the gray columns of smoke from the black ships as they powered toward the shore over 150 years ago.

It was a pleasure to visit these locations and just walk the grounds where larger-than-life people and events altered the world and the course of history.

26

EMBRACE THE CULTURE

When I was living in Hawaii, I enjoyed meeting people from many other countries and states who came to live and work there. A few of them didn't assimilate well, they liked the scenery but they weren't receptive to the lifestyle, they didn't eat the food and they were critical of Hawaii's people. For example, they criticized Hawaiian style 'plate lunches' and after all Hawaii is a 'plate-lunch' loving State. Others embraced the lifestyle, they ate the 'Ono' (delicious) food and socialized with the people. They did not assimilate totally nor need to, but their attitude was admirable. I may be guilty at times of being critical of other cultures but I aspire to have the same open attitude in Japan.

In Nippon, it is worthwhile to sample the cuisine, visit the festivals and temples, learn the culture, speak a bit of the language and mix with the people. At the same time, we can keep our identity including our own ideas, opinions , food and lifestyle. Acceptance of another culture can only enrich us.

EMBRACE THE CULTURE TEST

1. Do you eat Japanese food often? (Canned tuna doesn't count, raw tuna does)
2. Do you socialize with Japanese? (body to body on the packed rush hour train isn't the type of embracing or socializing I'm talking about)
3. Do you speak some Japanese? (Karaoke is Japanese if you pronounce 'Kaday-ookay')
4. Do you study culture, history or the lifestyle?
5. Do you follow the customs? (men walking first through the door as is customary here counts for half a point. I know these are liberated, modern times but why not let the lady walk first!)
6. Do you try to look on the bright side of living here?

Of course, if most of your answers are 'yes', then you pass.

SIX WAYS TO ENJOY THE CULTURE

- Visit the your local shrine and temple – every area has them. Keep in mind they are very busy on New Year's Day.
- Join the community Japanese language class – it is free, fun and you can meet other foreigners.
- Go on a ramen noodle hunt- hugely popular noodles are always on TV and in magazines. Find the best one and enjoy. Or eat at all of them. Go ahead stuff yourself!
- Ride the bullet train – It is quiet and smooth. Go to another prefecture and at the same time see the countryside.
- Make some Japanese friends and have a Nabe party – it's a party where everyone sits around a hot pot of vegetables and meat, and eats and drinks.
- Climb Mount Fuji. Then you can tell everyone 'Mount Fuji, been there. I started climbing at…'

27

CONCLUSION

Overcompensating grunts bombed the room as the chunky, sleeveless, alpha-male hopeful heaved another barbell over his hot head. On the cushioned mat, a pair of svelte thirty-something housewives stretched and posed in total silence. They had nothing to prove only fitness to gain. Such too was my goal as I found myself among this threesome one fine afternoon. Without ease, I did a rep of deltoid flies with an immaterial clank and inaudible huff trying as much as possible to use the correct form.

It was my day off and I usually went to the community gym because it cost 310 yen for two hours and had modest yet adequate equipment. I would exercise to the point of near exhaustion, which for me wasn't long, or I wouldn't feel quite satisfied.

Hunger now decided my next task so I headed to the nearby beef bowl shop. The picture-buttoned, food-ticket machine sucked in my 1000-yen bill and then spat out a pastel ticket. At the counter of mostly casually dressed men, I sat and tossed my stub on to the counter. The waitress grabbed it and within 2 minutes, she brought me; 1) a bowl of white rice crowned with fatty shoyu beef and onions, 2) a shredded cabbage, carrot and corn salad, 3) miso soup with clothy, flat, green seaweed and strips of fried tofu and 4) luke-cool water. Many Japanese add strips of red pickled ginger or a raw egg to the beef but I pass. 97% of the customers gobble, gulp and gallop after 3 minutes but I take an eternity and mosey on out after 20.

Almost content, I walked to the local library and settled into a good how-to book. Between chapters, my mind drifted into nostalgic reveries and I reminisced and though about the days and travels of this life's chapter.

- ❏ Long ago and far away I lived, learned, loved and worked on the Hawaiian Islands in the middle of the sea and have always considered them my home and will return one day to grind their gravy-filled plate lunches, swim at their sun-soaked beaches and walk their breezy streets.
- ❏ America is a free country and a booming economic powerhouse and it has a diverse population and a variety of cultures (34 million Americans are foreign-born). It has stunning earthly and man-made beauty ranging from the architecture of Manhattan to the natural ruggedness of the Colorado Rockies and from the brown, red and green colors of Arizona's Sonoran desert to the breaking surf at

Waikiki Beach. America is a great country and we can work and live our entire lives on its precious soil. As beautiful as it is, it's also true that one year abroad can enrich and add some spice to that potpourri of life.

- As Americans, we are free, free to choose where and how to live and America will always welcome us back. At immigration in Honolulu Airport, the officials give US citizens priority. Usually, the immigration officer says 'Welcome back!" What a great feeling! It is easy to travel; we can always go home.

- Like some fantastic novel or futuristic movie, in which an individual's action alters time and destiny forever, I hope that my life in Japan affected other lives positively. Maybe a student of mine was able to pass a test or use English effectively in another country. Maybe a friend gained a touch of optimism for having known me. For those students have actually taught me and those friends have actually added optimism and warmth to my life.

- A few years ago, I wrote an article for a publication. It was about Japan being like a paradise. A few years later, life here has remained great. To be truthful and objective, it hasn't been perfect. For example, my apartment has been broken into (nothing was taken) and I have been shortchanged and about ten immigration officers (one with a metal baton) came into my apartment at 6:30 a.m. with a pass key to check my passport. My passport was in order so they left quietly. Despite these things, I still believe many Japanese people are very kind and helpful - from friends, company staff to the person on the street. One day I went to Tsukigi fish market and on the platform, I asked a girl for directions. She gave them to me. They turned out to be wrong. Somehow, I don't know how, she found me again 10 stations down the line on a crowded platform and corrected the directions she gave me earlier. Later during the same trip, I asked a businessman for directions and he showed me the wall map. Then he ran to the station office and ran back with a small map of the area and explained about the district. Still later on the same day, in Tsukigi district, I asked for more directions from another man. He said he would show me the way. I felt very welcome that day near the fish market.

- The Western teaching management at my school has been fantastic. They always give so much support. My fellow teachers have always helped me and we always share a good laugh.
- Everywhere we go, we can find good people.
- For those of you who aspire to live or work in Japan, plan, prepare, believe in yourself and walk with confidence! Do the best you can and it is enough. YOU CAN DO IT! And whatever your dream is, I hope you find it.
- Being as amateur philosopher, I usually stick some words to live by, on my refrigerator. Currently, I have these words.

- ❖ Strive to do our best. If we can't, do it anyway. We can't be perfect and it is good to get things done. We only have so much time and we can try again.
- ❖ Don't worry - A higher power decides what we can't control.
- ❖ Help others (Love means helping someone).
- ❖ Enjoy and appreciate something everyday.
- ❖ Live courageously.

November A.M. Greater Tokyo Area

Darkness stalls as it reluctantly concedes to the impatient, juvenile rays of the pre-dawn, morning light. While chilly birds in an irregular, V-shape pattern fly south, brown, yellow and orange leaves show off their seasonal hues in celebration of autumn. Fresh, frosty air is kept at bay by the fuzzy warm blankets that hug my re-energizing flesh and bones.

Seconds tick slowly but life moves fast and soon it is mid-morning. My emotions and body, which unite like a band of sleepy brothers debate with my mind whether or not to leave the cozy heated perfection of my bedding. Alas, knowing any time on earth is indeed a generous and fleeting gift, too precious to squander, I climb out of my futon as slowly and surely as the sun rises from the early morning sea and begin another day.

ACKNOWLEDGMENTS

Thanks to my super editors from Canada, Iowa, England, Texas and California. You are much wiser than I am. Thanks to the kind people who participated in the surveys or offered their opinions. My family and friends always offer me support. Thank you. Many thanks to the Japanese staff and students who made my stay enjoyable. Finally, I would like to thank the teachers and teaching management who worked, drank and laughed with me.

ABOUT THE AUTHOR

Christopher Kona Young was born and raised in Honolulu, Hawaii where he ran around barefooted and worked in a pineapple factory during his high school summers. He had a 'squid-eye' (the ability to see hidden octopuses on the reef) and likes to eat kalua pig (Hawaiian underground smoked pork). His major at the University of Hawaii was accounting. During his career, he has worked as a Certified Public Accountant and computer programmer in Hawaii and California. He enjoyed a short stay in New York City. In Japan, he has taught English for several years. Recently, he has married his Japanese girlfriend. They live in the greater Tokyo area with their can of luncheon meat.